Information and Digital Literacies

Information and Digital Literacies

A Curricular Guide for Middle and High School Librarians

Lesley S. J. Farmer

ROWMAN & LITTLEFIELD
Lanham • Boulder • New York • London

Published by Rowman & Littlefield
A wholly owned subsidiary of The Rowman & Littlefield Publishing Group, Inc.
4501 Forbes Boulevard, Suite 200, Lanham, Maryland 20706
www.rowman.com

Unit A, Whitacre Mews, 26-34 Stannary Street, London SE11 4AB

British Library Cataloguing in Publication Information Available

Library of Congress Cataloging-in-Publication Data

Farmer, Lesley S. J.
Information and digital literacies : a curricular guide for middle and high school librarians / Lesley S.J. Farmer.
pages cm
Includes bibliographical references and index.
ISBN 978-1-4422-3980-7 (hardback : alk. paper) — ISBN 978-1-4422-3981-4 (pbk. : alk. paper) — ISBN 978-1-4422-3982-1 (ebook) 1. Information literacy—Study and teaching (Middle)—United States. 2. Information literacy—Study and teaching (Secondary)—United States. 3. Computer literacy—Study and teaching (Middle)—United States. 4. Computer literacy—Study and teaching (Secondary)—United States. 5. School librarian participation in curriculum planning—United States. 6. School librarians—Effect of technological innovations on—United States. 7. School libraries—Information technology—United States. I. Title.
ZA3075.F35 2016
028.7071—dc23
2015022403

To my California professional colleagues and students

Contents

Preface

Early on in my school librarianship career, I aimed for a systematic way to make sure that all of the students that I served became information literate. It didn't seem fair that students' competency would depend largely upon the goodwill and time that individual classroom teachers might have to plan with me. Nor did I find a satisfactory curriculum, or even a good list of K–12 library skills (the forerunner of information literacy terminology).

Even today, many school librarians encounter the same problem. School librarians can locate thousands of lesson plans related to information and digital literacies, but systematic scope-and-sequence curricular are harder to find. Commercial and nonprofit agencies are now providing streamlined digital safety stand-alone curriculum, but they usually are adopted as supplementary learning experiences, offered in a vacuum separate from the required curriculum. For students to gain information and digital literacy competence, they must have meaningful, content-rich learning experiences so that process and product are intertwined authentically. Furthermore, these learning experiences must be integral to the school's curriculum.

Therefore, no ready-made standardized curriculum, textbook, and prescribed instruction and assignments can fit the bill. Instead, school librarians need to collaborate with the rest of the school community to analyze and reform the school curriculum to integrate information and digital competencies meaningfully in order to meet the needs of the students. Content and its engagement must be developmentally appropriate and articulated appropriately in order to optimize spiral learning and reinforcement.

This book provides a framework to design and implement information and digital literacy curriculum for middle and high school communities. Chapter 1 gives an overview of the evolution of literacy, education, and school librarianship. Chapter 2 details information literacy, and chapter 3 details digital literacy. Chapter 4 examines students' information and digital needs and behaviors. Chapter 5 explains instructional design, and chapter 6 suggests ways to integrate information and digital literacies into the curriculum. Chapter 7 provides a model information and digital literacies curriculum for middle school, and chapter 8 provides a similar curriculum for high school; these curricula offer a starting point for school librarians to use as they collaborate with their school communities.

A case may be made that the future lies in the hands of school librarians. They have the knowledge, skills, and dispositions to optimize the acquisition and use of information and digital literacies by students. And these students will need those literacies to improve their worlds—and the conditions for society. Few vocations are as powerful.

Chapter One

Introduction

How do we prepare today's K–12 students for a tomorrow that we can only imagine? The world is ever changing. Information constantly grows—and changes itself, especially as technology facilitates its creation and dissemination by an ever-broadening population base. With advancing technology, people are more likely to come into contact with each other and with that changing information. How do students make sense of this world, and how will they make future worlds? In a knowledge society, today's K–12 students need to gain and create information in a myriad of ways, responding to needs. Information and digital literacies are needed now more than ever.

THE EVOLUTION OF INFORMATION

What do we mean by the term *information*? The easiest definition of information is meaningful data. While information has existed throughout human history, it has exploded in quantity and variety within the last century. Indeed, information has come to be regarded as a human right both in terms of physical and intellectual access. "Everyone has the right to freedom of opinion and expression; this right includes freedom to hold opinions without interference and to seek, receive and impart information and ideas through any media and regardless of frontiers" (United Nations, 1948, Article 19).

The nature of the information itself has been affected by digital technology. Besides the obvious combination of text, image, and sound, technology facilitates the repurposing and transformation of information in order to address different objectives or different audiences. More than ever, the user needs to interpret the format of information as well as its content. The interface between the information and the user consists of another element that has not been as crucial previously. For instance, hypertextuality enables the

1

reader to go to linked information that might be further linked to other documentation; while footnotes and bibliographies serve this purpose hypothetically, they generally do not provide instant connections to the referred content. That same interface also gives rise to interactive and dynamic information. Applications such as Google Docs and wikis enable participants to literally change documents on the fly, thereby chipping away at the idea of a permanent recorded document.

THE EVOLUTION OF LITERACY

Literacy constitutes a pillar of education. The ability to read and write, to use language effectively, is required in today's society. Literacy is not an intuitive skill; it requires conscious and deliberate learning and practice. The explosion of technology calls for increased literacy skills, and technology can also be used to teach those literacy skills.

A simple definition of literacy is the ability to use written language purposefully: the ability to read, write, spell, listen, and speak. However, how literacy is operationalized has changed over the centuries. For instance, reading a known text such as the Bible was the basis for being literate at one point; the emphasis was on recall. That kind of literacy expanded to the ability to read an unknown text. Similarly, writing as part of literacy expanded from the ability to copy a known text to producing an original document. With a changing world, the idea of passing down knowledge to replicate is seriously outdated. While students continue to need to consume information knowledgably, they also need to produce new knowledge.

What educational experiences ensure these literate abilities? Theoretically, once they learn how to read and comprehend mathematical thinking, students should be able to learn on their own. Or can they?

It is not enough to comprehend a text; a student could read inaccurate information but not realize its falseness. Such knowledge comes with subject-domain experience, but with so much information now available, no one can possibly have the background to be acquainted with all of the topics encountered. Critical thinking is required so that students can use logic and other evaluative strategies to discern the veracity and perspective of the new information that they encounter. More generally, today's literacy involves the ability to access, engage, use, and share a wide spectrum of information: to be information literate.

Furthermore, students need to reflect on their learning, identifying what strategies work and what learning gaps remain. They can also reflect on their feelings while learning. In either case, they can determine next steps. This metaliteracy is, in essence, literacy about literacy. It is the basis for learning how to learn.

THE EVOLUTION OF EDUCATION

Education needs to prepare K–12 students for this ever-expanding world, providing youth with the intellectual tools and competences to survive and lead the future. However, most curricula continue to be arranged by academic domains so that learning processes are sometimes integrated unsystematically. Furthermore, learning experiences themselves manifest sometimes conflicting educational philosophies, and they tend to reflect current and past societal realities rather than presage future possibilities.

To be fair, educational practices have diversified in this century. While lecturers remain as a viable way to share narrative information, digital storytelling and multimedia presentations, among other resources, enable students to access information using multiple senses. Notes continue to provide a means for students to extract and comment on information, but the forms of note-taking, including taking photos, has greatly expanded. High-stakes standardized testing has threatened to "flatten" curriculum and bring back rote learning. However, constructivist learning activities and inquiry-based projects offer alternative and active ways to engage with the curriculum.

Likewise, delivery modes of education have also expanded, even in K–12 settings. While field trips have declined in number overall, virtual field trips and online guest speakers have risen significantly. Increasingly, students take Advanced Placement courses online. School configurations have diversified: block scheduling for longer learning sessions, differentiated class period lengths to align with learning experiences (e.g., short discussion periods versus long science labs), career pathways, small thematic learning academies, community college courses before high school graduation, schoolwork combinations, senior capstone experiences, and so on. The line between formal and informal education is beginning to fade.

As with information processes, educational practices have been impacted by technology. Teachers have complemented textbooks with other information sources for hundreds of years and have incorporated audiovisual resources for over a century. However, the Internet has opened the floodgates of information and enabled students to access ideas globally. Students can demonstrate their learning in many more formats, particularly through technological tools: from microscopes to probes, from cameras to webcams, from simulations to apps.

THE EVOLUTION OF SCHOOL LIBRARIANS

As information professionals, school librarians have the expertise and are uniquely positioned to teach information and digital literacies across the academic curriculum, independently and in collaboration with the rest of the school community.

These roles have evolved over the years. Most library services in U.S. schools were started as outreach efforts by public librarians, who brought resources to the school sites. Resources continue to serve as the focal point for school libraries, with physical access as the core function.

Over the years, school librarians have expanded their services to include intellectual access through instruction on research skills. As more states required teaching preparation and practice as part of the school librarian credential, instructional roles expanded: as information consultants, partners, and collaborators. Throughout these library program configurations, school librarians have continuously served the entire school community across the curriculum.

Similarly, school librarians have increasingly leveraged technology in their work, from typewriters to integrated library management systems. When audiovisual education emerged in the 1950s, some school libraries were renamed as media centers, and some school librarians served as media specialists. School librarians produced media products such as audio slideshows and transparencies, and later they created videos and web pages. School librarians routinely gained skill in productivity applications, and some school librarians learned advanced technology skills such as netware and programming. As instruction gained prominence in school library programs, school librarians have spearheaded the integration of technology in teaching and learning. With the advent of the Internet, school librarians introduced digital resources and software into schools and now are incorporating social media into the mix. This development also necessitated teaching students how to locate and evaluate online resources, because school library collections were no longer completely under the selective control of the librarian. The new Makerspace Movement further pushes the active participatory role of students in the library program specifically and the overall mission of the school.

THE EVOLUTION OF INFORMATION AND
DIGITAL LITERACIES CURRICULUM

As a result of these changes in school libraries, education and society as a whole, school librarians realize the growing importance of information and digital literacies. At state, national and international levels, school librarians and other educators have developed standards for information and digital literacies. However, their curricular role within the school community has not been as well recognized or established.

Learning about information and technology differ from learning *with* information and technology. Melding information and digital literacy has been uneven and has usually been used in order to facilitate access to resources and project production. Schools have offered technology courses for generations, typically using a tool-based skills approach. More recently, technology-based courses have focused on projects, such as media courses to create a video school "yearbook" or content-centric web design courses. Courses about information have tended to focus on skills too, such as bibliographic instruction and study skills. Studying about the nature of information and how to engage with it has seldom been addressed systematically.

With new national and state standards for content, as well as information and digital literacies, the time is right to develop an articulated scope-and-sequence curriculum that melds these standards. However, curriculum needs to align with district and site-specific missions and goals and should reflect the needs and interests of its school community. Thus, an intellectual tension exists between these two mind-sets. As a feasible approach, curriculum planners as a whole can particularize the general standards by specifying the standards' indicators and learning activities in the context of their community.

Fortunately, because they work with all grades and content areas, school librarians are well positioned to partner with the school community to develop and implement such a curriculum. Those school librarians with teaching expertise, in particular, can be seen as instructional partners. In addition to instructing the curriculum content, school librarians can also provide the conditions for optimum learning: an inviting and stimulating learning environment, a rich collection of resources, and trained staff to provide supportive services.

REFERENCE

United Nations. (1948). *Universal declaration of human rights*. Paris, France: United Nations.

Chapter Two

Information Literacy

The classic definition of information literacy speaks to the individual's ability and habit to access, evaluate, use, manage, generate, and communicate information effectively and responsibly. Several new standards have updated and reconceptualized information literacy and 21st-century learning: the American Association of School Librarians (AASL), the Association of College and Research Libraries (ACRL), the International Federation of Library Associations and Institutions (IFLA), and the Partnership for 21st Century Learning. Although not specifically mentioned, information literacy is a fundamental set of skills in the Common Core State Standards as well. This chapter describes emerging thinking about information literacy and provides concrete examples at different grade levels. The school librarian's role in addressing information literacy is also detailed.

DEFINING INFORMATION LITERACY

As the definition of literacy changed over centuries, the need to address the broader idea of information engagement became evident. Library skills presaged information literacy, focusing on how to use the library. Such user education, sometimes called bibliographic instruction, taught students how to locate, cite, and use library resources, especially reference materials such as encyclopedias and atlases. Instruction was tool based and skills based.

The term *information literacy* was first used publicly in 1974 by Zurkowski in his report to the U.S. National Commission on Libraries and Information Science. He couched the idea in terms of a person's use of primary sources and information tools to solve problems. The 1989 American Library Association Presidential Committee on Information Literacy stated that "to be information literate, a person must be able to recognize when information is needed and have the ability to locate, evaluate, and use effectively the needed information" (p. 1). With this philosophy, instruction needed to be more open ended and student centric because the individual defined the information need. Nevertheless, information literacy tended to be conflated with research skills, which results in the undervaluation of a person's use of information literacy competence to respond to immediate imposing information, such as the sound of a flat tire.

While librarians spearheaded these efforts, the need for information literacy transcends librarians. As early as the U.S. Department of Labor's 1991 *SCANS* (*Secretary's Commission on Achieving Necessary Skills*) report, governmental agencies have noted the need for employees who can locate, interpret, and organize information; communicate information; create documents; solve problems; work with a variety of technology; and know how to acquire new knowledge. At the international level, the 2003 World Summit on the Information Society (WSIS), governments and world leaders "made a strong commitment towards building a people-centred, inclusive and development-oriented Information Society for all, where everyone can access, utilise and share information and knowledge" (United Nations, 2003, p. 1).

Defining information literacy continues to challenge librarians and other stakeholders. In their 2007 *Standards for the 21st Century Learner*, AASL included in their common beliefs that information literacy has become more complex because of the expanded kinds of resources and that the term *information literacy* should be complemented by more specific literacies, such as digital and visual literacies.

UNESCO (the United Nations Educational, Scientific and Cultural Organization) and IFLA renamed information literacy as "information and media literacy" (MIL) in order to explicitly highlight the importance of format as the "container" for information, with the understanding that the medium helps shape the information. They defined MIL as

> a set of competencies that empowers citizens to access, retrieve, understand, evaluate and use, create, as well as share information and media content in all formats, using various tools, in a critical, ethical and effective way, in order to participate and engage in personal, professional and societal activities. (UNESCO, 2014, p. 18)

For its part, ACRL has also grappled with the definition of information literacy as evidenced by its task force, who revised the 2000 ACRL information literacy standard; the task force's definition of information literacy grew cumbersome as it tried to capture the concept's richness and complexity. Their current definition follows.

Information literacy is a spectrum of abilities, practices, and habits of mind that extends and deepens learning through engagement with the information ecosystem. It includes:

- understanding essential concepts about that ecosystem;
- engaging in creative inquiry and critical reflection to develop questions and to find, evaluate, and manage information through an iterative process;
- creating new knowledge through ethical participation in communities of learning, scholarship, and civic purpose; and
- adopting a strategic view of the interests, biases, and assumptions present in the information ecosystem. (Association of College and Research Libraries, 2000, p. 12)

INFORMATION LITERACY STANDARDS

Standards provide a way to operationalize information literacy, to identify what students need to know and be able to do if they are information literate. At its core, information literacy standards address access, evaluation, use, and communication of information. Nevertheless, as with definitions of information literacy, specific associated standards have changed in response to external changes such as technology advances and globalization.

American Association of School Librarians

AASL (2007) sidestepped the problematic term *information literacy* when it used learners as its linchpin; they stated that

learners use skills, resources, & tools to:

1. Inquire, think critically, and gain knowledge.
2. Draw conclusions, make informed decisions, apply knowledge to new situations, and create new knowledge.
3. Share knowledge and participate ethically and productively as members of our democratic society.
4. Pursue personal and aesthetic growth. (American Association of School Librarians, 2007, p. 3)

Each standard is then parsed into specific indicators that demonstrate learner skills, dispositions in action, responsibilities, and self-assessment strategies. For example, within the standard about using knowledge is the skill of organizing knowledge so that it is useful, the disposition of adapting information strategies flexibly, the reponsibility of connecting understanding to the real world, and the self-assessment strategy of reflecting on systematic processes. Furthermore, AASL lists developmental and grade-specific indicators in their follow-up 2009 publication. Building on the above example,

- Grade 2 uses word processing and drawing tools to organize information.
- Grade 5 uses various technology tools to retrieve and organize information.
- Grade 8 uses appropriate media to develop products that show understanding.
- Grade 12 delivers a professional presentation to an external audience.

The AASL standards are predicated on common beliefs, which serve as preconditions for the learning standards: reading, inquiry-based learning, explicitly taught ethical behavior, technology skills, equitable access, expanding information demands, social context of learning, and the importance of school libraries. The last belief underscores the role of school libraries vis-à-vis information literacy: convenient equitable access to rich resources and collaborative instruction and practice in using these resources.

In sum, AASL sees its standards as:

- A comprehensive vision for student learning in libraries
- Consistent with school district vision
- Compatible with National Educational Technology Standards and 21st Century Skills
- Preparing students for a future of change.

Association of College and Research Libraries

Academic librarians also run into the stumbling block of the term *information literacy*, particularly since it wasn't in general parliance at the time of many professors' own academic preparation. Academians seem to be more comfortable with the terms *critical thinking* (which usually refers to the ability to comprehend and analyze a given document but which excludes the ability to locate relevant and worthy documents) and *research skills* (which does not address the ability to respond to unintended information problems).

This latter concept of research skills largely drove the 2000 ACRL information literacy skills, which address information needs, access and evaluation, incorporation of information into one's knowledge base, purposeful use, and ethical/legal issues.

As did AASL, ACRL (2015) reconceptualized information literacy and its associated standards. The librarians who constituted the ACRL task force to revise information literacy standards embraced the notion of developing expertise and recontextualized information literacy as a set of threshold concepts that would characterize the domain of information literacy. They developed six "frames" or intellectual "lenses" by which to consider information literacy:

- Authority is constructed and contextual
- Information creation as a process
- Information has value
- Research as inquiry
- Scholarship as conversation
- Searching as strategic exploration (ACRL, 2015)

Each frame includes a description of the concept, followed by knowledge practices (which can be considered as representative indicators), dispositions, and sample learning activities and assessments. For example, under the frame of searching, one knowledge practice is using different types of appropriate searching language, and one disposition is understanding that first attempts at searching do not always produce adequate results. Academic librarians are intended to reflect on these frames and use them to drive deep conversations with academic communities about the nature of information literacy and how to help students understand and apply these concepts within and across academic domains.

UNESCO

As noted above, UNESCO and IFLA joined the concepts of information and media since format and ideas have a symbiotic relationship. As with ACRL, UNESCO (2014) avoided the term *standards*, preferring the term *competencies* couched within an assessment framework. They defined competency as

> the ability of an individual to mobilize and use internal resources such as knowledge, skills and attitudes, as well as external resources such as databases, colleagues, peers, libraries, tools, and instruments, among others, in order to solve a specific problem efficiently in a real-life situation. (UNESCO, 2014, p. 55)

UNESCO (2014) then parsed media and literacy competencies into three components:

- Access and Retrieval: "Recognizing the demand for, being able to search for, being able to access and retrieve information and media content"
- Understanding and Evaluation: "Understanding, assessment and evaluation of information and media" (includes organization)
- Creation and Utilization: "Creation, utilization and monitoring of information and media content" (includes participation in societal-public activities) (p. 57)

Each component is made up of of four competencies with associated indicators demonstrating knowledge, skills, and attitudes/values/rights, parallel to the work of AASL and ACRL.

Partnership for 21st Century Learning

The Partnership for 21st Century Learning (http://p21.org) is an influential coalition of leaders in education, business, and public policy who address student readiness. To this end, they created a framework for student outcomes, which has been widely accepted. Besides core subjects (the three Rs and thematic domains), the partnership posited the need for life and career skills, the four Cs of learning and innovation skills (critical thinking, communication, collaboration, and creativity), and information media and technology skills. The latter cluster includes information literacy, media literacy, and information communications technology (ICT) literacy. The overall characteristics include access to information, technology, critical thinking, collaboration, and contributing to society. Its information literacy component includes accessing, evaluating, using, and managing information; the component also references AASL.

The Partnership for 21st Century Learning (2011) also developed indicators for 4th, 8th, and 12th grades in order to show the developmental aspects of their framework. Information and media literacy indicators are provided within three academic contexts: English, social studies, and mathematics (http://www.p21.org/our-work/resources/for-educators#SkillsMaps).

Common Core State Standards

The Council of Chief State School Officers and the National Governors Association developed the 2010 Common Core State Standards (CCSS), largely as a way to measure student performance across state lines in response to the federal Race to the Top educational plan. The goal of the standards is to identify what students need to know and do in order to be college and career ready by the time they graduate from high school. As such, the CCSS focus on English language arts and mathematics in terms of critical thinking, research, application, communication, and technology. The 2012 Next Generation Science Standards (NGSS) align with and complement the CCSS, adopting the CCSS dimensions of content and practice, cutting across traditional science domains.

In terms of progression, the CCSS list indicators for each grade Kindergarten–6 and Grades 7–8, 9–10, and 11–12. For instance, in terms of reading standards, the progression includes: Recognize common types of texts (e.g., storybooks, poems, fantasy, realistic text), which is reflected in the following grade ranges.

K–1. Compare storybooks and informational books.

2. Use text features to locate key facts.

3. Identify a main idea in a text, and recount key details that support the main idea.

4. Interpret presented information visually, orally, or quantitatively.

5. Locate an answer to a question using multiple print or digital sources.

6. Read and comprehend literature, including stories, dramas, and poetry.

7–8. Conduct short research projects to answer a question, using several sources.

9–10. Analyze in details how an author's ideas or claims are developed.

11–12. Evaluate the effectiveness of an author's structure in his exposition or argument.

The NGSS standards include specific science domain and thematic benchmark content and indicators at Grades 2, 5, 8, and 12.

Even though information literacy is not explicitly referenced, the concepts are reinforced as the CCSS emphasize deep and broad reading and the ability to write and research and use media technology for analysis and production. Likewise, the NGSS also incorporate information literacy concepts and skills:

> The core ideas also can provide an organizational structure for the acquisition of new knowledge. Understanding the core ideas and engaging in the scientific and engineering practices helps to prepare students for broader understanding, and deeper levels of scientific and engineering investigation. (Board on Science Education, 2012, p. 24)

California Model School Library Standards

In the United States, standards for information literacy and school libraries are state specific. In 2011, the California State Department of Education approved the California Model School Library Standards (CMSLS). These standards were the result of a provision within the state education code, which permitted the development of library standards. The state Library Consultant and California School Library Association members drew upon the standards of AASL and the International Society for Technology in Education (ISTE), as well as the CCSS, in order to create four information literacy concepts:

- *Students access information.* The student will access information by applying knowledge of the organization of libraries, print materials, digital media, and other sources.
- *Students evaluate information.* The student will evaluate and analyze information to determine what is appropriate to address the scope of inquiry.

- *Students use information.* The student will organize, synthesize, create, and communicate information.
- *Students integrate information literacy skills into all areas of learning.* The student will independently pursue information to become a lifelong learner. (California State Department of Education, 2011, pp. 8–9)

Each concept included general indicators, followed by grade-specific knowledge, skills, and dispositions.

Cross-Walks

As is apparent in examining these standards, they largely align with each other. Variations occur mainly in terms of indicators for specific grade levels. The UNESCO and ACRL standards have a broader scope, largely because they pay more attention to the nature of information itself. In attempts to show how information literacy is embedded in the CCSS, school librarians have created cross-walks between their information literacy standards and the CCSS. Here are a couple of examples:

- http://www.ala.org/aasl/standards-guidelines/crosswalk
- http://schools.nyc.gov/NR/rdonlyres/1A931D4E-1620-4672-ABEF-460A273D0D5F/0/EmpireStateIFC.pdf
- http://k12digitalcitizenship.wikispaces.com/For+Librarians

With these cross-walks, school librarians can collaborate more easily with classroom teachers and explicitly include information literacy student learning outcomes into lesson plans.

IMPLICATIONS FOR SCHOOL LIBRARIANS

To ensure that all students have adequate opportunities to become information literate, a systematic approach is needed. Librarians are the logical point persons since they work with all students and all curricular areas and witness the developmental aspects of learning. They can act as institutional representatives and catalysts, aware of student and faculty needs, practices, and parameters.

To that end, school librarians should first become familiar with relevant information literacy standards, including cross-walk documents that can help "translate" information literacy terms into the vocabulary of each discipline. School librarians should also brainstorm resources and learning activities that would exemplify these standards. With that knowledge base, school librarians can then work with their school communities to advance the conversation about information literacy expectations and the roles that librarians can play. These conversations can inform curriculum development and deployment.

REFERENCES

American Association of School Librarians. (2009). *Standards for the 21st century learner in action.* Chicago, IL: American Library Association.

American Association of School Librarians. (2007). *Standards for the 21st century learner.* Chicago, IL: American Library Association.

American Library Association Presidential Committee on Information Literacy. (1989). *Final report.* Chicago, IL: American Library Association.

Association of College and Research Libraries. (2015). *Framework for information literacy for higher education.* Chicago, IL: American Library Association.

Association of College and Research Libraries. (2000). *Information literacy competency standards for higher education.* Chicago, IL: American Library Association.

Board on Science Education. Division of Behavioral and Social Sciences and Education. National Research Council of the National Academies. (2012). *A framework for K–12 science education.* Washington, DC: National Academies Press.

California State Department of Education. (2011). *Model school library standards for California public schools: Kindergarten through grade twelve.* Sacramento: California State Department of Education.

Council of Chief State School Officers and the National Governors Association. (2010). *The Common Core State Standards for English language arts & literacy in history/social studies, science, and technical subjects.* Washington, DC: Common Core State Standards Initiative.

Partnership for 21st Century Skills. (2011). *Framework for 21st century learning.* Washington, DC: Partnership for 21st Century Skills. http://www.p21.org/storage/documents/1._p21_framework_2-pager.pdf

UNESCO. (2014). *Global media and information assessment framework: Country readiness and competencies.* The Hague, Netherlands: UNESCO.

United Nations. (2003). *Declaration of principles. Building the information society: A global challenge in the new millennium.* Paris, France: United Nations.

U.S. Department of Labor. (1991). *Secretary's Commission on Achieving Necessary Skills (SCANS).* Washington, DC: Government Printing Office.

Zurkowski, P. (1974). *The information service environment—Relationships and priorities.* Washington, DC: U.S. Commission on Libraries and Information Science.

Chapter Three

Digital Literacy

Digital literacy, technology skills, information and communications technology (ICT) competence. These terms all deal with electronic content and the tools used to engage with them. Technology has certainly impacted society and to some extent, education. For students to be contributing citizens to society, they need to know how to handle these technologies, which means that schools should prepare students accordingly. This chapter discusses how technology competency has changed over the recent decades, noting current International Society for Technology in Education (ISTE) and International Technology and Engineering Educators Association (ITEEA) standards, as well as ways that digital literacy is incorporated in Common Core and information literacy. The school librarian's role in addressing digital literacy is also detailed.

TECHNOLOGY IN SOCIETY

Today's society has been called the Information Age and the Knowledge Society. Those attributions have brought them with a number of issues: information overload, quicker change, the potential for more participatory democracy, globalization, a greater sense of both isolation and community, as well as a tension between standardization and personalization. Regardless of individual perceptions about technology, its impact has grown over the last half century. Noting the importance of technology in society, the U.S. Department of Education as early as 1983, in its report *A Nation at Risk*, contended that

> the people of the United States need to know that individuals in our society
> who do not possess the levels of skill, literacy and training essential to this

new era will be effectively disenfranchised, not simply from the material re-
wards that accompany competent performance, but also from the chance to
participate fully in our national life. (p. 6)

Technology has certainly changed in recent decades. Prior to the 1980s,
technology was largely associated with government and corporations using
large-scale equipment to transmit one-way communication via broadcasting
or to crunch numbers for science and business. Just thirty years ago, a Super
Bowl ad heralded the downfall of Big Brother with the introduction of the
Macintosh computer. Even looking back to 2001, one finds mobile devices
and iPods just being introduced; social-networking sites were just appearing.
YouTube and Blu-ray weren't launched until 2005, and Twitter started only
in 2007.

This century has witnessed significant expansion of multimedia information and online services, be it commercial or governmental. Technology has
accelerated globalization and heralded the relative democratization of technology with the potential for widespread participatory sociopolitical engagement. Indeed, the rise of crowdsourcing and collective intelligence testify to
the power of drawing upon diverse expertise in order to achieve economic
and cultural advancement together, transcending the limitations of any one
person (Friedman, 2005).

At the same time, people can feel ever more overwhelmed by information, unable to discern among the vast quantities of uneven quality information, let alone deal comfortably with myriad gadgets and applications. Those
who communicate online sometimes do not realize the extent and permanen-
cy of their efforts. Especially as people's digital presence can impact their
lives, it is imperative to know how to manage technology effectively and
responsibly.

TECHNOLOGY IN STUDENTS' LIVES

Sometimes young people do not realize the extent and impact of technology.
Students might consider technology to be a convenient way to shop, to keep
in touch, or to be entertained, but they might not realize the economic and
social implications of technology on their world—and their place within it.

Online information and instruction enables students to learn what they
want and need to learn outside of school strictures and social prejudice, and it
expands their economic futures. The Internet provides anonymity and auton-
omy—and at the same time that it jeopardizes privacy, it offers personalization. The Internet has the added advantage of being interactive, so students
can control how they retrieve information, they can connect with experts in
the field, and they can get appropriate feedback that helps them learn more
effectively and efficiently. Students in need can get access to public agencies

and take advantage of translation programs. Furthermore, the Internet offers a global venue to express oneself; students can present their ideas with a professional look by learning how to do desktop publishing. Web-based learning can also help students connect with a new set of peers, thus extending their social network.

In sum, technology impacts teenagers in their daily and future lives, even if they are not fully aware of technology's reach.

TECHNOLOGY IN SCHOOLS

Yet even when today's students take technology gadgets and interactive Internet features for granted, they may have limited access to these digital tools inside of school. This picture is changing with the advent of the Common Core State Standards, which stipulate that students need to use technology tools to gain and demonstrate knowledge, including use for standardized testing. Even with well-maintained labs and a solid collection of digital resources, learners will not profit from technology-enhanced activities if educators do not provide related learning opportunities.

For the most part, the chief reason that technology is not used to improve learning is lack of knowledge on the part of the educators themselves. Most of them are digital immigrants and have not experienced a technology-rich academic setting themselves. Many educators use technology on a personal basis, such as for communication, but have not had formal training in technology-integrated instructional design. Therefore, many do not feel comfortable using such educational technology in the classroom or online.

Interestingly, both children and adults are likely to have learned how to manipulate today's technology informally: from friends and family, from online tutorials and help desks, or by simply "messing around" themselves. In that respect, generations have a near-level playing field when it comes to learning new technologies. Nevertheless, librarians and other educators cannot assume that students or teachers know how to use technology for academic purposes. Librarians, even in higher education, testify to students' unsophisticated use of search engines and databases.

DEFINITIONS OF TECHNOLOGY AND DIGITAL LITERACY

The basic idea of technology literacy is the ability to use technology effectively and responsibly, including applying it in novel situations and generating knowledge with it. However, as technology has changed radically in the last generation or two, so too has the definition and terminology of technology changed.

The terms *technological literacy* and *technology literacy* started out focusing on the performance aspect of literacy, "how to use a particular piece of technology" (Belshaw, 2011, p. 73). Early discussion about this literacy avoided issues of societal judgment about technology usage.

Computer literacy tended to focus on computer benefits, including skills that could help prepare one for the workplace. Computer programming was one aspect of computer use but not considered required for literacy, although programming would demonstrate computer fluency (Nevison, 1976). By the 1990s, computer literacy focused more on the use of applications to access and create knowledge rather than to build computers or networks. Interestingly, coding has regained attention, this time focusing on the concept of logical thinking.

At the beginning of the 21st century, the term *ICT literacy* gained a foothold, especially in Europe. This literacy encompassed applications use, online engagement, and e-learning. According to the Educational Testing Service ICT Literacy Panel (2002), ICT literacy was supposed to have a more conceptual basis, rather than be limited to procedural skill; in Europe, ITC was more skills based. Furthermore, ICT literacy is sometimes used instead of the term *information literacy* in order to describe a set of competencies. In other words, no common understanding arose.

The term *digital literacy* first gained public recognition with Gilster's 1997 book, *Digital Literacy*. Gilster (1997) emphasized the metacognitive nature of digital literacy in his discussion: "The ability to understand and use information in multiple forms from a wide range of sources when it is presented via computers" (p. 2). The American Library Association (2013) defined digital literacy as "the ability to use information and communication technologies to find, evaluate, create, and communicate information, requiring both cognitive and technical skills" (p. 2). In his synthesis of research literature on digital literacy, Belshaw (2011) posited eight elements of digital literacy:

- Cultural: understanding digital contexts
- Cognitive: using a set of cognitive technology tools
- Constructive: creating with technology
- Communicative: understanding how communications media work
- Confident: understanding problem-solving
- Creative: doing new things in new ways
- Critical: reflecting on digital practices in various semiotic domains
- Civic: using technology to support and develop civil society (i.e., digital citizenship)

Because technology continues to change and our engagement with it also changes, it is likely that the definition of digital literacy will continue to evolve. However, school librarians can work within the current reality to help students become digitally literate.

TECHNOLOGY LITERACY STANDARDS

It should be noted that learning *about* technology differs from learning *with* technology. The former focuses more on the nature of technology itself, such as the operations of a computer or network. The latter focuses more on ways that technology helps to gain and demonstrate content knowledge, such as using a microscope to see cell structure; it is an intellectual means to an end, rather than an end in itself. Generally, career and technology education tends to be more tool based, although it does explore the societal and social purpose of technology. Learning with technology may be integrated across all curricula.

As noted in chapter 2, some organizations combine information and technology literacy standards. For instance, UNESCO and the International Federation of Library Associations and Institutions (IFLA) developed information and media literacy standards with the idea that media convey information. Similarly, the Partnership for 21st Century Skills clusters together information media and technology skills. In its introduction of its 21st-century learning standards, the American Association of School Librarians (2007) considered technology as a learning tool rather than a subject of study; thus, it mentions technology within its standards in terms of the format of mastering technology tools to access, analyze, organize, and communicate information in different media.

International Society for Technology in Education

The most popular technology literacy standards were developed by ISTE, an international nonprofit organization of education and technology leaders and their affiliated groups. ISTE (2007a) identified six areas of competency:

- Creativity and innovation
- Communication and collaboration
- Research and information fluency
- Critical thinking, problem solving, and decision making
- Digital citizenship
- Technology operations and concepts

As noted in chapter 2, these competencies tie well to information literacy, the main difference being in technology operations, which is a necessary skill for accessing much information.

ISTE's (2007b) *Profiles for Technology (ICT) Literate Students* provides benchmark indicators for Grades 2, 5, 8, and 12. For instance:

- By Grade 2, students can navigate e-books and websites.
- By Grade 5, students can collaborate with digital-planning tools.
- By Grade 8, students can solve routine hardware and software problems.
- By Grade 12, students can design a website.

International Technology and Engineering Educators Association (formerly International Technology Education Association)

As the subtitle of its standards—"content for the study of technology"—indicates, ITEEA promotes technology education for all, with a strong emphasis on STEM (science, technology, engineering, and mathematics; International Technology Education Association, 2007). Its five standards address

- the nature of technology, such as its core concepts
- technology and society, such as technology's effects on the environment and society
- design, such as engineering design and experimental problem solving
- the designed world, such as technologies used in different industries
- abilities for a technological world, such as using and maintaining technology products and systems

Similarly to ISTE, ITEEA provides benchmark indicators for Grades 2, 5, 8, and 12. However, the descriptions are much more detailed. For instance, Grades K–2 should learn how vaccinations protect people from getting some diseases. ITEEA's standards can easily be the framework for technology education curricula.

Common Core State Standards

As noted in chapter 2, the Common Core State Standards (CCSS) embed digital literacy into the standards. Among other educational entities, the Fresno County Office of Education (n.d.) extracted the technology standards from the Common Core content standards as follows:

- Reading text standard 7 (several genres/subjects) and speaking/listening standard 2: Integrate and evaluate content presented in diverse formats.
- Reading information text standard 5: Analyze text structures.
- Reading literacy in sciences standard 9: Analyze and compare texts by theme and author approach.

- Writing standard 2 (several subjects): Write informative/explanatory texts through effective selection, organization, and analysis of content.
- Writing standard 6 (several subjects): Use technology to produce writing and collaborate.
- Writing standard 8 (several subjects): Gather relevant information from multiple print and digital sources, assess their credibility and accuracy, and integrate the information.
- Speaking and listening standard 3: Evaluate speaker's point of view, reasoning, rhetoric, evidence.
- Speaking and listening standard 5: Use digital media and visual displays of data to express information.
- Language standard 4: Determine or clarify vocabulary by consulting resources.

Basically, technology used to locate information, gain knowledge, produce knowledge, and collaborate.

The Next Generation Science Standards (NGSS) also refer to technology use in the manner stated above, but science-specific technology tools such as microscopes and probes are incorporated and to greater depth.

California Model School Library Standards for Technology

Technology literacy standards are integrated into California's 2011 Model School Library Standards, reflecting the philosophy that this literacy largely overlaps or is a prerequisite skill for information to be accessed and used effectively. For instance, students need to know how to turn on a computer and access an Internet browser in order to locate a book in the library or use an online database. Here are some sample indicators of technology literacy in these standards:

- *Students access information:* Students access information by applying their knowledge about digital media organization.
- *Students evaluate information:* Students evaluate and analyze digital information to determine appropriateness in addressing the scope of inquiry.
- *Students use information:* Students use a variety of technology tools to organize, synthesize, create, and communicate information.
- *Students integrate information literacy skills into all areas of learning:* Students independently pursue online information to become lifelong learners. (California State Department of Education, 2011)

DIGITAL CITIZENSHIP

Digital literacy usually mentions the need to use technology responsibly: legally and ethically. For instance, ISTE lists digital citizenship as one aspect of digital literacy, focusing on responsible and productive use. However, digital citizenship has gained separate attention, largely because of irresponsible online behavior such as plagiarism, piracy, and cyberbullying.

Digital citizenship may be defined as the ability to use technology safely, responsibly, critically, productively, and civically. The overarching goal is effective and responsible personal and social engagement with digital resources for learners. While some of the motive is protection and safety, which has resulted in required filtering software and acceptable use policies, a more positive spin is the need for learners to learn coping skills and demonstrate that they can contribute meaningful knowledge to the digital society.

Four national sets of recent standards reinforce the need for digital citizenship, informing teacher librarians and the rest of the educational community. The 2007 ISTE National Education Technology Standards for Students address technological responsibility (ISTE, 2007a). Likewise the Standards for the 21st Century Learner developed in 2007 by the American Association of School Librarians asserts that "ethical behavior in the use of information must be taught" (p. 2). Several of the 2010 Common Core standards reiterate the need for digital citizenship across the curriculum in terms of responsible use, attribution and citation practices, and online safety issues (Council of Chief State School Officers and the National Governors Association, 2010). The Partnership for 21st Century Skills (2013) couches digital citizenship in terms of reimagining citizenship: navigating and participating in the digital world safely and responsibly as a global citizen.

The typical elements of digital citizenship include the following, which use Ribble (2011) as a basis:

- Protection: digital security, digital health and wellness, digital rights and responsibilities, digital reputation
- Respect: digital access, digital etiquette, digital law
- Education: digital literacy, digital communication, digital commerce/consumer awareness and behavior, digital civic engagement/contribution

Civic education itself has been losing ground in education, so it is not surprising that digital citizenship has not been embraced except as a means to keep children safe and crime free (i.e., not plagiarize, steal, or bully); the proactive element is usually missing. Not only should librarians and classroom teachers develop a systematic curriculum, but the educational community also needs to model digital citizenship in its infrastructure and actions: providing equitable access to digital information, making provisions to ensure that the educational community is digitally safe, having a plan to secure and protect educational data in case of crime or disaster, maintaining privacy and confidentiality of individual records, creating and enforcing policies that protect the digital rights of everyone, and training staff in order to keep them current in digital citizenship education.

IMPLICATIONS FOR SCHOOL LIBRARIANS

School librarians are well positioned to teach all youth—and the rest of the school community—about how to access, process, and share information in myriad forms for myriad purposes, incorporating the effective and responsible use of technology. School librarians also know that digital literacy is most effective when addressed explicitly with authentic and meaningful tasks, such as improving health, within the context of valued curricula. When teaching and promoting digital citizenship, school librarians need to make learners aware of digital citizenship issues, engage learners in grappling with those issues, and guide learners in ways to solve those issues, such as social justice.

Here are a dozen ways that librarians can teach and promote digital literacy, including digital citizenship, within the community:

1. Serve on curriculum development and professional development committees.
2. Contribute to school and district technology plans (which, among other reasons, are required for e-rate discounts).
3. Survey the school community about their physical access to technology.
4. Provide in-school and remote access to digital resources.
5. Circulate technology, such as e-readers, camcorders, and mobile devices.
6. Produce and disseminate webliographies about digital literacy, including digital citizenship.
7. Provide face-to-face and online instruction on the evaluation and selection of digital resources.
8. Provide face-to-face and online instruction to the school community on using technology as a learning tool.
9. Explain to the school community about intellectual property and ways to give people credit for their ideas.
10. Promote the Creative Commons (http://creativecommons.org) and contribute to its database of documents.
11. Teach the school community about cyberbullying and ways to respond to such bullies.

12. Support and supervise youth social networking and podcast productions (e.g., book talks, library promotions, tech tips).

REFERENCES

American Association of School Librarians. (2007). *Standards for the 21st century learner.* Chicago, IL: American Library Association.

American Library Association, Office for Information Technology Policy. (2013). *Digital literacy, libraries, and public policy.* Chicago, IL: American Library Association.

Belshaw, D. (2011). *What is digital literacy? A pragmatic investigation* (doctoral dissertation). Durham University.

California State Department of Education. (2011). *Model school library standards for California public schools: Kindergarten through grade twelve.* Sacramento: California State Department of Education.

Council of Chief State School Officers and the National Governors Association. (2010). *The Common Core State Standards for English language arts & literacy in history/social studies, science, and technical subjects.* Washington, DC: Common Core State Standards Initiative.

Fresno County Office of Education. (n.d.). *Technology standards.* Fresno, CA: Fresno County Office of Education.

Friedman, T. (2005). *The world is flat.* New York: Farrar, Straus and Giroux.

Gilster, P. (1997). *Digital literacy.* New York: Wiley.

ICT Literacy Panel. (2002). *Digital transformation: A framework for ICT literacy.* Princeton, NJ: Educational Testing Service.

International Society for Technology in Education. (2007a). *International educational technology standards for students.* Eugene, OR: International Society for Technology in Education.

International Society for Technology in Education. (2007b). *Profiles for Technology (ICT) literate students.* Eugene, OR: International Society for Technology in Education.

International Technology Education Association. (2007). *Standards for technological literacy: Content for the study of technology* (3rd ed.). Reston, VA: International Technology Education Association.

Nevison, J. (1976, October 22). Computing in the liberal arts college. *Science, 396*–402.

Partnership for 21st Century Skills. (2013). *Reimagining citizenship for the 21st century.* Washington, DC: Partnership for 21st Century Skills.

Ribble, M. (2011). *Digital citizenship in schools* (2nd ed.). Eugene, OR: International Society for Technology in Education.

U.S. Department of Education. (1983). *A nation at risk.* Washington, DC: Government Printing Office.

Chapter Four

Students and Literacy

What do students need to know and do in order to become information and digitally literate? This chapter looks at today's students and the socioeconomic context of their lives. The chapter will examine students' information behaviors and highlight their learning needs with respect to information and digital literacies. The chapter also explains issues that impact students' literacy learning: human development and maturity, gender, cultural contexts, and special needs. The librarian's role in dealing with students vis-à-vis information and digital literacies concludes the chapter.

PROFILES OF TODAY'S STUDENTS

Today's generation of students, most of whom were born in this century, are sometimes called the G generation because of their interaction with Google or games or green technology. They have largely grown up with social media and apps, dealt with high national security, taken high-stakes standardized tests, and are one of the most diverse generations in the United States.

Developmental Issues

When teaching information and digital literacy, school librarians and other educators have to remember that they are instructing students who are still developing physically, mentally, and psychologically. The brains of many boys, for instance, do not develop formal logic capabilities until age fourteen, so expecting these students to apply abstract concepts to novel situations is unrealistic. Even the assumption that all middle school students are functionally literate in terms of reading may be inaccurate.

As youth progress from preteen to emerging adult, they are striving to become self-sufficient and meaningfully connected with others. During this time, youth develop a personal value system, gain a more complex perspective on life, assume more responsibilities, make more decisions, and deal with their own bodily and emotional changes. In the process, they take intellectual, physical, and social risks while experimenting with different aspects of themselves and their environment.

Middle schoolers represent a broad spectrum of maturity, from late childhood to early adulthood in terms of bodily, emotional, and cognitive changes. Even within one preteen different aspects of maturity can be witnessed, such as childlike thinking in a mature body. Additionally, within a single day, emotions can run the gambit from calm assurance to temper tantrums and anxiety. It is no wonder that many middle schoolers live in the "now," and may neglect to consider the consequences of their actions. Middle schoolers tend to be self-conscious, and at the same time they want to be accepted and liked by others. Both conformity and bullying peak at this point. These years, ages 12 to 14, mark the tipping point at which time peers become more important to them than their parents. On the whole, girls tend to be more mature than boys at this age and may be in the throes of social messages that push certain prescribed female expectations that were not as strident in earlier developmental stages, such as bodily images and social roles.

Younger teens are becoming more independent as they negotiate the more complex structure of high school and its increasingly diverse student population. These 14- to 16-year-olds often have high self-expectations but may still suffer from poor self-esteem. They may feel a sense of loss as their relationships with their parents change, and at the same time they look forward to deeper peer group connections. These teens are also starting to think about their futures in terms of postsecondary options, career choices, and sexuality.

Older teens have a more realistic self-concept and a more stable personality than preteens, and they are dealing with more complex life choices, including sexual issues. They can think abstractly and independently and take pride in their work. They are likely to realize and accept social institutions and adult responsibilities. Perry's (1999) research on the cognitive development of college students applies to many high schoolers. He posited that students transcend from a dualistic worldview (authority-based right or wrong) to multiplicity as they encounter diverse ways of thinking. Multiplicity tends to focus on process and may "flatten" the comparative veracity of ideas. The next stage, relativism, suggests that most knowledge is contextual and relativistic and evidence is needed to support opinions. The ultimate stage is commitment, of making—and being responsible—for life choices based on considering alternatives.

Youth at Risk

Growing up is challenging, even for an adept young person. Fortunately, most teens weather the developmental "storms" with resilience. The Search Institute (2007) in Minneapolis identified 40 external and internal development assets that help youth stay resilient. Youth need caring support and positive models from family, neighbors, and other adults in their lives. Schools and community organizations need to communicate clear boundaries and expectations and provide opportunities for youth to be engaged in learning, service, and self-expression. Youth who lack resiliency are often, not surprisingly, disconnected for a substantial amount of time. This conscious sense of disconnect is felt mainly by older teens who have to make life decisions and assume adult responsibilities.

Teens at risk tend not to have the safety nets over a substantial period of time to help them resolve "outside" crises successfully. To further explain this situation, one can use the analogy of being "broke" to being poor: the former is short term, the latter is a substantive condition. Such youth tend to experience at least one of the following over time: poverty or welfare status, lack of one or two parents, undereducated parents, personal academic failure, personal parenthood, drug abuse problems. Youth may feel disconnected at school because of cultural factors, such as values and language, that differ from the dominant school culture. Furthermore, teens who migrate have to renegotiate social expectations and relationships as they make new connections.

It should also be realized that youth with disabilities are more likely to experience academic or social challenges than typical teens. They may experience different ways of accessing, processing, or expressing information. Because disabilities vary so much, even within one set of disorders, such as autism, librarians need to individualize instruction and learning activities in order to accommodate differences.

HOW STUDENTS LEARN

Several processes need to occur in order for students to learn. True learning only takes place if some change occurs; if the information just reinforces current knowledge, then no new learning happens. Students have to become aware of the content and be stimulated to pay attention. They need to engage with the content information and process it. They need to comprehend the content and make meaning of it. They then can relate the content to their current knowledge and determine what to do with it: reject it, integrate it into their existing knowledge base, use it, or communicate it.

Throughout these steps, individual students vary in their processes depending on their own biology and personality as well as their context. For instance, Sternberg (1985) posited three approaches to internal processing: analytical, creative, and contextual. Howard Gardner's (1983) theory of multiple intelligences suggests difference "lenses" to learning. The Myers-Briggs Type Indicator focuses on personality traits that impact engagement with information. Kolb's (1984) learning-style dimension contrast concrete to abstract thinking and observation versus experimentation. Furthermore, individuals have different learning-space preferences in terms of time of day, sound and visual stimuli, and physical setup.

Like human development, learning is developmental: dependent on changing physiology, growing self-awareness, and an expanding base of experience and knowledge. Thus, learning starts by being based on concrete experience and later can include abstract thinking and generalization. As youth mature, they are more able and more likely to share their expertise. Ethical and moral aspects of learning change from externally based rules to internal value systems. With maturity, students can also be more self-reflective and can regulate their own learning.

STUDENTS' EDUCATIONAL ENVIRONMENT

Students' formal and informal educational environment reflects several tensions: standardization versus differentiation of instruction, individual accountability versus collaborative learning, back-to-basics versus career tracks, content centric versus student centric. Even within one school, students may experience significant differences in instructional approaches and learning activities.

The school library presents a mix of formal and information education in that not all content or learning activities are prescribed. Resources and services lend themselves to different means of engagement. It should also be noted that the quality of school library programs varies widely across the nation—and even within one district. These differences occur because of legislation and funding, as well as district and school culture, all the way to the individual school librarian. Access may be very open—all day to groups and individuals; alternatively, it may be available for limited hours to a limited population. Resources typically support the curriculum but may also address students' personal interests. Some school libraries are print heavy while others are approaching digital only. Programming such as storytelling and events occur more often in elementary libraries, although gaming and literature circle activities peak in middle school, and tutoring services could be provided at any level. The amount and quality of instruction also vary, as does the nature of librarian-teacher collaboration. Student participation ranges from library aides to social or service clubs; some high school libraries have student advisory boards and work-study options.

STUDENTS' INFORMATION BEHAVIORS

What kinds of information are young people seeking? Agosto's (2011) summary of young adults' information needs provides a good starting point for consideration:

- Relationships (family, peers, etc.)
- Other emotional needs
- Health and safety, including sexuality
- Academics, including college
- Careers/jobs
- Recreational and leisure interests
- Popular culture
- Consumer needs

How do youth satisfy their information wants and needs? As do other searchers of all ages, youth first ask family, friends, and likely information experts (Foss, 2014). Likewise, youth start where they were successful before, staying within their information literacy comfort zone. Often they are unaware of specialized reference sources or online subscription article databases either because they have not been given associated instruction—by the school or by public librarians—or because they do not have access to such resources due to libraries' financial constraints. As students mature, they seek a wider spectrum of research and favor digital sources over print ones (Purcell et al., 2012). Nevertheless, they may still favor quantity over quality. As a result, students may get information that they cannot comprehend or information that doesn't answer the research question (Savolainen & Kari, 2004). In terms of their searching strategy, teens tend to use unsophisticated methods. Even the notion of keywords eludes some preteens and teenagers (Branch, 2001).

Age accounts for much of the differences in information behaviors: in terms of academic and personal needs as well as competency. For instance, information seeking requires higher cognitive and metacognitive skills. Personal and familial background and experiences impact the development of knowledge structures and interactions with one's environment. Lu (2010) also noted that children develop a sense of control as they mature and are more likely to seek information if they think that they have some power to control the situation; children are also more likely to think that the information found is more useful if the information need is under their control.

Teens' brains are still developing, particularly in term of formal abstract-logic abilities and values system (Dobbs, 2011). Thus, they might not make logical assumptions or think through their decisions to their logical consequences with the result that they do not pace themselves realistically when conducting research or realize that they may get caught plagiarizing. When those negative consequences occur, then teenagers' neural circuits overload, activating swinging emotional moods and spiraling them down further. At the same time, the brain is wired to encourage risk taking, so librarians should leverage this tendency by facilitating intellectual risk taking.

Context also impacts students as they evaluate the source: What is the perspective? How accurate is it? How thorough is it? How useful is it for the purpose of solving the problem? Students sometimes do not give a critical eye to resources and instead consider any piece of information as "holy script," particularly if it is found online. Students might not consider the perspective of the author or understand the context of the information. For instance, a scientist is likely to have a different perspective than a religious leader when discussing stem-cell research. Fortunately, today's youth are becoming more information savvy. In testing 11- to 17-year-olds' ability to detect good and bad information, Flanagan and Metzger (2010) found that students realize the negative consequences of believing false information, and they pay close attention when the information need is highly valued. Students tend to overestimate their ability to critically and accurately evaluate websites; younger students tend to be less trustful of websites, but older students are more concerned about the quality of information. In another "bright-spot" study, which investigated how youth evaluate information, Gasser et al. (2012) culled the following criteria used: topicality, relevance (i.e., match with the intended purpose), utility, significance, credibility, domain name (e.g., .edu and .gov are preferred to .com websites), popularity, amount of information, visual attractiveness, interactivity, peer opinion, and personal preference.

Agosto (2011) also synthesized researchers' identification of barriers experienced in youths' information behaviors. Some barriers rest with the searcher: lack of subject knowledge, lack of knowledge about how to locate and use source material, discomfort with the information task or the information itself (e.g., not wanting to know about spiders), feeling overwhelmed by information or the task, social discomfort, and negative feelings about libraries or librarians. Other barriers are external to the youth: access barriers and other use restrictions such as library closures, lack of available resources, lack of access to technology, and lack of transportation. Gasser et al. (2012) added the challenges of information complexity and distractions. Still other barriers have been identified: lack of language, literacy, technology, and research skills, as well as lack of motivation and low valuation of an imposed information task.

STUDENTS' TECHNOLOGY USE

According to the U.S. Census figures for 2013 (File & Ryan, 2014), 84% of households own a computer, and three fourths are connected to the Internet, with 92% of minors having computer access or 81% of minors having Internet access. Three quarters of children ages 8 and younger have access to some "smart" device (Common Sense Media, 2013). According to Madden et al. (2013), 93% of teens have access to a computer, and older girls tend to access the Internet via cellphone. Asian and White metropolitan households with high incomes and high educational achievement are most likely to have technology and Internet access. Poor rural Blacks in the South have the least access. Teens on the fringes of digital technology also tend to be on the educational and societal fringes, as noted above. Ideally, technology can be an effective means to empower teens within their favored culture as well as provide a means to connect with other groups, particularly those with socioeconomic power. Teens can improve themselves and can work with others to reach an ideal (Keeble & Loader, 2001).

Youth tend to use computers for entertainment: social networking, e-games, and videos (Rideout, Foehr, & Roberts, 2010). More recently, the activity of searching for information has become more popular (Feierabend & Rathgeb, 2012). It must also be acknowledged that some young people do not balance their technology lives and become addicted to Internet use or e-gaming, which can lead to mood disorders and unhealthy living (Wartberg et al., 2014). On the other hand, technology also helps teens' information behavior; teens can access relevant resources from around the world and choose materials that fit their learning preferences.

Gender also impacts technology access and use. Girls tend to see technology more as a tool, while boys see it as a toy. Girls use the Internet more than boys but spend less time online on average than boys; parents also allowed boys more time than girls to use computers (although girls tended to use the time allotted and boys overstayed their time). Boys are more likely than girls to use digital technology for entertainment; girls are more likely to use the Internet for information seeking and socializing. Boys also report more self-confidence using technology than girls (Wang et al., 2012). In terms of Internet use for academic purposes, girls were more likely to be negatively affected by socializing, while boys were negatively affected by e-gaming (Chen & Fu, 2009).

Libraries constitute teens' main organizational conduit for freely accessing technology, largely because of their convenience, hours of operation, and neutral stance. In addition, online library information services can give teens more control as they can choose when to ask for help and can "hide" behind the computer interface, thus minimizing feelings of vulnerability. About a third of teens use libraries in order to access the Internet. Two thirds of those library Internet users did research and browsed the Internet for entertainment, a small majority used e-mail, 47% got health information, 41% got government information, 36% looked for jobs, a third visited social-networking sites, and a quarter watched videos (Zickuhr, Rainie, & Purcell, 2013).

Physical access to technology is a precondition for its use, but teens also need procedural and conceptual knowledge in order to use technology: mechanical technical operations, searching techniques, comprehension and evaluative skills, data manipulation skills, and communication skills. All too often, teens learn these skills through trial-and-error exploration rather than through formal training (Foss, 2014). As a result, many teens unrealistically think that they are tech savvy and can find their way around the Internet. However, teens often overlook valuable information in favor of easy "hits." They might not understand what they are accessing—the authorship, the perspective, the underlying message. Even when teens find the information they want, they might not know what to do with it. Continuing brain development also impacts technology use since teens may know how to do technical tasks such as creating and downloading digital information but might still struggle with realizing that they should not take that action (e.g., flaming others, pirating music). Therefore, librarians need to explicitly teach responsible use, scaffolding teens' moral decision-making processes. In researching preteen and teen research behaviors, Purcell et al. (2012) interviewed teachers, who asserted that digital search tools have advantaged students but that these tools also contributed to students' "surface" searching and short attention spans.

The following truisms culled from Lien (2000), Lubans (1999), and Vansickle (2002) reflect teens' attitudes about online technology use.

- Wikipedia is king.
- Google is awesome.
- Want news? Go online.
- Social networking is good for homework.
- Instant messaging is better than e-mail; e-mail is so yesterday—it's for old people and teachers.
- If information isn't on the front page, it probably isn't worthwhile anyway.
- "Good enough" is good enough.
- Free is good.
- Downloading is OK as long as you're not selling it.
- I get scared sometimes, but I can take care of myself.

IMPLICATIONS FOR SCHOOL LIBRARIANS

As school librarians design information and digital literacy instruction, they must first consider the interests, needs, developmental capabilities, and contexts of their student population. The more that school librarians can know about their students, the more effective their interaction and instruction can be, building on internalized motivation. For their part, the more self-aware students are, the easier it is for them to relate to information. School librarians should also teach metacognitive skills so that students can self-monitor and regulate their information behaviors, thus controlling their own learning to a greater extent.

To optimize student engagement with information, school librarians should provide choices: of resources to use, learning activities, and ways to demonstrate literacy. To this end, school librarians should strive for strong collections of developmentally appropriate materials in various formats. The library itself should also offer a variety of learning spaces and ways to interact with information.

School librarians should not assume that students know how to use technology for academic purposes. To optimize learning, school librarians should provide explicit instruction and learning support through scaffolding, opportunities for peer coaching through collaborative projects, and appropriate accommodations for students with linguistic differences or special needs.

REFERENCES

Agosto, D. (2011). Young adults' information behavior: What we know so far and where we need to go from here. *Journal of Research on Libraries and Young Adults, 2*(1). Retrieved from http://www.yalsa.ala.org/jrlya/2011/11/young-adults%E2%80%99-information-behavior-what-we-know-so-far-and-where-we-need-to-go-from-here/

Branch, J. (2001). Information-seeking processes of junior high school students. *School Libraries Worldwide, 7*(1), 11–27.

Chen, S., & Fu, Y. (2009). Internet use and academic achievement: Gender differences in early adolescence. *Adolescence, 44*(176), 797–812.

Common Sense Media. (2013). *Zero to eight: Children's media use in America 2013.* San Francisco, CA: Common Sense Media.

Dobbs, D. (2011). Beautiful brains. *National Geographic, 220*(4), 37–59.

Feierabend, S., & Rathgeb, T. (2012). Media usage behaviour of adolescents in Germany. *Media Perspektiven, 43*(6), 339–352.

File, T., & Ryan, C. (2014). *Computer and Internet use in the United States: 2013.* Washington, DC: U.S. Census Bureau.

Flanagan, A., & Metzger, M. (2010). *Kids and credibility: An empirical examination of youth, digital media use, and information credibility.* Cambridge, MA: MIT Press.

Foss, E. (2014). *Internet searching in children and adolescents: A longitudinal framework of youth search roles.* Dissertation, University of Maryland.

Gardner, H. (1983). *Frames of mind: The theory of multiple intelligences.* New York: Basic Books.

Gasser, U., Cortesi, S., Malik, M., & Lee, A. (2012). *Youth and digital media: From credibility to information quality.* Cambridge, MA: Berkman Center for Internet & Society.

Keeble, L., & Loader, B. (2001). *Social capital and cyberpower.* London: Routledge.

Kolb, D. (1984). *Experiential learning: Experiences as the source of learning and development.* Englewood Cliffs, NJ: Prentice-Hall.

Lien, C. (2000). Approaches to Internet searching: An analysis of student in grades 2 to 12. *Journal of Instruction Delivery Systems, 14*(3), 6–13.

Lu, Y. (2010). Children's information seeking in coping with daily-life problems: An investigation of fifth- and sixth-grade students. *Library & Information Science Research, 32,* 77–88.

Lubans, J. (1999). When students hit the surf: What kids really do on the Internet. And what they want from librarians. *School Library Journal, 45*(9), 144–147.

Madden, M., Lenhart, A., Duggan, M., Cortesi, K., & Gasser, U. (2013). *Teens and technology 2013.* Washington, DC: Pew Research Center.

Perry, W. (1999). *Forms of intellectual and ethical development in the college years.* San Francisco, CA: Jossey-Bass.

Purcell, K., Rainie, L., Heaps A., Buchanan, J., Friedrich, L., Jacklin, A., Chen, C., & Zickuhr, K. (2012). *How teens do research in the digital world.* Washington, DC: Pew Internet & American Life Project. Retrieved from http://pewinternet.org/~/media//Files/Reports/2012PIP_TeacherSurveyReportWithMethodology110112.pdf

Rideout, V., Foehr, U., & Roberts, D. (2010). *Generation M2: Media in the lives of 8- to 18-year-olds.* Menlo Park, CA: Kaiser Family Foundation.

Savolainen, R., & Kari, J. (2004). Placing the Internet in information source horizons. *Library and Information Science Research, 26,* 415–433.

Search Institute. (2007). *40 developmental assets for adolescents.* Minneapolis, MN: Search Institute. Retrieved from http://www.search-institute.org/content/40-developmental-assets-adolescents-ages-12-18

Sternberg, R. (1985). *Beyond IQ: A triarchic theory of human intelligence.* Cambridge, MA: Harvard University Press.

Vansickle, S. (2002). Tenth graders' search knowledge and use of the web. *Knowledge Quest, 30*(4), 33–37.

Wang, L., Luo, J., Gao, W., & Kong, J. (2012). The effect of Internet use on adolescents' lifestyles. *Computers in Human Behavior, 28*(6), 2007–2013.

Wartberg, L., Kammerl, R., Sonja Bröning, S., Hauenschild, M., Petersen, K., & Thomasius, R. (2014). Gender-related consequences of Internet use perceived by parents in a representative quota sample of adolescents. *Behaviour & Information Technology.* doi:10.1080/0144929X.2014.928746

Zickuhr, K., Rainie, L., & Purcell, K. (2013). *Library services in the digital age.* Washington, DC: Pew Research Center.

Chapter Five

Literacy Curriculum and Instructional Design

This chapter explains how to develop an information and digital literacies curriculum. Starting with identified desired learning outcomes, librarians determine the content of the curriculum to be delivered and what learning activities give students the opportunity to learn and demonstrate competency. Assessment should be considered at this starting point. Then librarians can identify the material and human resources needed to implement the curriculum; several useful curricular resources will be listed. Next, librarians have to decide how to deliver the curriculum; a number of possible configurations are provided. Issues of time, space, technology, and personnel are addressed.

WHAT DO SCHOOL LIBRARIANS NEED TO KNOW?

The previous chapters provide a sound basis for developing a curriculum: definitions of information and digital literacies, standards and benchmark indicators, and profiles of today's students.

According to the National Council for Accreditation of Teacher Education (NCATE, 2008), beginning teachers need to demonstrate the following competencies, which tie to instructional design:

- "Select instructional strategies and technologies, based on research and experience, that help all students learn" (NCATE, 2008, p. 2).
- Construct learning experiences that "support individual students' development, acquisition of knowledge, and motivation" (Association for Childhood Education International, 2007, p. 1).

- Understand, integrate, synthesize, and teach content knowledge, skills, and dispositions.
- Use a variety of teaching strategies to encourage students to develop critical thinking and problem-solving skills.
- Foster active student engagement in learning and social interaction.
- Effectively assess for instruction and make adjustments to positively impact student learning.
- Model reflective practice in light of research.
- Collaborate professionally with the school community and local agencies.

Around the world, teacher preparation programs see the need for entering teachers to use information and communications technologies for personal use and as a tool for learning, particularly as globalization has shrunk intellectual borders and social media has become a mainstay for many students. More specifically, in the United States, the Common Core State Standards (CCSS) also require students to handle information more deeply and use technology to learn and demonstrate competence.

Fortunately, most school librarians have teaching expertise, so they understand the principles of pedagogy. They know how students learn and can set up the conditions for optimum interaction—with content, peers, and instruction—and gaining knowledge. School librarians should also have a good idea about ways to manage and assess student activity and learning, as well as assess instruction. Additionally, most school librarians know how to select appropriate resources for curricula.

As school librarians design instruction, they need to know how to contextualize that instruction in light of the school community. To that end, school librarians need to understand the school's mission and vision, recognize the school's culture and educational philosophy, be acquainted with the student population and its demographics, and analyze the school's curriculum in light of information and digital literacies. School librarians also need to know the school teaching faculty and be able to collaborate with them. Education is fundamentally a social construction, not an abstract, one-size-fits-all boilerplate experience. Only with knowledge of the educational context can school librarians design and manage instruction that support the school community—and is valued by that school community.

THE CURRICULUM

At its most basic level, the curriculum may be considered as the content matter that students are expected to know and apply. Standards inform the curriculum. Indicators operationalize the standards so that educators have criteria that specify performances that demonstrate the degree to which a student has met the standard. Determining that content and how to convey it so that students will learn the content constitutes instructional design.

The curriculum and its development may occur on several levels: from a single learning activity to teach a specific skill to a school-wide or even an international curriculum (e.g., an international baccalaureate program). The curriculum might be initiated by a single individual (e.g., a school librarian) all the way up to an international consortium. In all cases, the curriculum builds on need and should consider and align the following factors. The phrases in italics provide examples from a potential information literacy curriculum.

- Target learner population: *kindergartners, math teachers*
- Learning activity: *critiquing an advertisement, creating a digital story*
- Course (be it a single session or a sequenced series of related student learning outcomes): *workshop on MLA citation style, unit on intellectual property, digital citizenship course*
- Program (curriculum for a well-defined academic domain): *language arts, information literacy*
- Institutional mission: *school site*
- System or consortium: *district*

Information literacy often has difficulty finding a spot in most schools' curricula. Historically, students might have taken a course or unit on library skills or research skills. Most school librarians think that information literacy should not be a separate course or sequence of learning activities separate from an academic domain because information literacy processes need to engage meaningful information. On the other hand, the case can be made that studying about information itself is a worthwhile academic endeavor, which might lead to the field of information science itself.

In a way, information literacy resembles the approach of the CCSS, which increasingly drive K–12 instruction. The CCSS initiators assert that the standards are not curricula; that tasks remains in the hands of school educators. So the case might be made that information literacy standards are not a curriculum per se. The latter standards are even "more slippery" because they are not tied to subject matter, which CCSS does to some degree. On the other hand, information literacy touches every academic subject, even if it is not recognized. At the very least, critical thinking—which includes the evaluation of resources—should constitute part of every subject matter.

In that regard, digital literacy lends itself more easily to the concept of a set curriculum because students can learn about technology and gain specific technology skills, such as web design and video editing. Furthermore, students are likely to work with technology in science classes, either as part of lab experiments or virtual simulations. In most cases, school librarians do not serve as technology teachers, instructing students in productivity applications or computer file management. On the other hand, school librarians do serve an important role in helping students with how to learn with technology: locating and evaluating digital resources, representing and organizing information using technology (e.g., spreadsheets, infographics), and communicating meaningfully about information by determining appropriate formats (e.g., blog, podcast). How that curriculum is determined and designed poses the same challenges as information literacy (under which these aspects of technology fall).

Therefore, school librarians tend to collaborate with other classroom teachers so that information and digital literacy competencies can be integrated with content-rich coursework. This cross-curricular situation results in difficulties deciding where information literacy fits within the school curriculum. Oftentimes research skills, which make up part of information literacy, are taught in English or social studies courses. However, that approach leaves out the sciences and the arts, which also figure into information literacy in terms of the scientific method, numerical data analysis, visual and aural literacies, and so on.

One approach is to develop a school-wide scope-and-sequence information and digital literacy curriculum map. The information and digital literacy standards can be listed and then assigned to a specific grade and subject, with the proviso that all students receive information and digital literacy instruction and practice in every grade and every required subject. Two chapters in this book provide such a structure.

INSTRUCTIONAL DESIGN

Instructional design is a systematic planning process to develop educational programs that align and interrelate content, activities, products, environments, and assessment. Instructional design acknowledges the learner's prior experiences and active engagement and situationally contextualizes instructional methods so that learning can meet desired outcomes. Theoretically, instructional design provides a predictable process and criteria for assessing its effectiveness and impact on learning.

Several instructional models exist, and ADDIE is the most popular one. Created for the U.S. Armed Forces (Branson & Rayner, 1975), it includes five design steps:

1. *Analysis*: of students' needs and current skills and the learning environment

2. *Design*: of strategies to help students meet identified outcomes, including content and its organization, delivery format, learning activities, and assessment
3. *Development*: of strategies "packaging" and pilot-testing of the instructional design
4. *Implementation*: of design, including instruction and activities
5. *Evaluation*: of learning, delivery, and instructional design

Another instructional model, ASSURE, explicitly addresses the integration of technology into the process (Smaldino & Lowther, 2011):

1. Analyze learners' general characteristics, current competencies, and learning preferences.
2. State objectives in terms of the target learner: behaviors, conditions under which to demonstrate learning, quality of competence, and context of the learning objectives.
3. Select strategies and materials, including technology, in light of objectives and learners.
4. Use materials to help learners meet objectives through preparing materials, learning environment, and learners.
5. Require learner participation through engagement, practice, and feedback.
6. Evaluate and refine instructional design in terms of its impact on student learning.

It should be noted that instructional design applies to all kinds of learning environments and delivery modes. Online tutorials, webinars, and even printed guidesheets are all possible instructional design products.

ANALYSIS

Just as in a journey, the ultimate destination is determined first, and so too does the student learning outcome need to be the starting point in instructional design. What do we want students to know and be able to do in order to be information and digitally literate? The existing information and digital literacy standards discussed in earlier chapters are predicated on answering this question and even provide indicators of competence. These outcomes vary in terms of the type of knowledge to gain and demonstrate (Hubbell, 2010).

• Declarative knowledge: facts, such as citation style or classification system

- Procedural knowledge: skills, such as locating an article or making a podcast
- Contextual knowledge: knowing when to apply knowledge, such as determining the kind of graphic organizer to represent concepts or the types of questions to raise in an interview
- Experiential knowledge: real-world applications, such as learning research skills for a debate or a science experiment

In designing instruction, school librarians need to identify the type of knowledge expected in order to develop discrete objectives that specify the behavior to perform, the quality of that action, and the conditions under which that behavior is assessed. In other words, objectives need to be SMART: specific, measurable, achievable, relevant, and time bound. For instance, "Given five titles of nonfiction books, within 5 minutes students write down the correct call number for each title using the OPAC."

The identified objectives then drive content, instructional strategies, learning activities, and assessment. For instance, learning citation style would typically call for direct instruction and practice producing accurate citations using real resources. In contrast, inquiry-based learning might be more appropriate for experiential knowledge.

Once the outcome is specified, instructional design analysis can focus on students and the learning environment. What is the level of information and digital competence of students currently? What is the literacy gap between their current status and the desired literacy status? What prerequisite knowledge and skills do they have? School librarians can gather data from existing school surveys, census figures, grades and test scores, observation, and discussions with the school community.

This exercise may lead to a task analysis. For instance, if the objective is for students to locate appropriate articles in an online database aggregator, students first need to be able to

- read and comprehend the subject matter, which requires reading literacy fluency and subject-matter vocabulary knowledge
- identify keywords and phrases, including synonyms
- spell accurately
- perform inputting actions (e.g., keyboarding, mouse use, touch screen manipulation)
- operate a computer
- access and navigate the Internet
- perform keyword and Boolean searching

Without these prerequisite skills, assessment of possible articles for selection will be waylaid. In that respect, developing a scope-and-sequence curriculum can optimize instruction because the school librarian can make assumptions about the likelihood that students have the necessary background to successfully learn and perform the task.

Of course, within a grade or class, students are likely to have different levels of skills and knowledge, so the instructional design needs to take those differences into consideration when determining the content to be included. Scaffolding, such as tutorials on search strategies or read-aloud text applications, may be needed. In some cases, the learning activity can be designed as a collaborative project so that students can peer coach as a way to get all of the students up to speed.

At the same time, school librarians should also determine the objective's assessment: both *what* is assessed and *how* it is assessed. A well-conceptualized objective simplifies this task; indeed, usually writing objectives and assessments go hand in hand. It should be noted that assessments can be used as a

- diagnostic tool at the beginning of a learning unit in order to identify preexisting knowledge and skills
- formative tool during instruction and learning in order to provide specific feedback and determine needed interventions
- summative tool after instruction in order to make decisions about learners and instructional design

A wide variety of assessment instruments exists. As school librarians select assessment instruments, they should consider

- validity: measuring the specific objective (e.g., counting the number of books a child checks out does not necessarily mean that the child read those books)
- reliability: getting the same result with the same instrument
- cost
- time: for development, use, and analysis
- legality

Table 5.1 includes a beginning list of possible instruments, noting advantages and disadvantages of each.

School librarians also need to analyze the learning environment, not only within the library but within the entire school. What facilities are available (e.g., labs, production areas, presentation venues)? How is space used? What technologies are available? What is the school time schedule, and how is time generally used? Where is the library located relative to classrooms? What is the school culture in terms of educational expectations and values?

Table 5.1.   Assessment Instruments

Assessment Instrument	Measures	Advantages	Disadvantages
Survey	Perception	Quick, easy, cheap	Self-reporting (might be inaccurate)
Test	Facts	Quick, easy, cheap, standardized	Needs to be carefully developed to be valid; most tests are costly; essays may be subjective
Visual product (e.g., drawing, time line, graphic organizer)	Process, skill, comprehension	Flexible, cheap	Might measure visual literacy and skills more than content knowledge; might be subjective
Video	Process; skill	Authentic (although editing may impact authenticity)	Time-intensive; might assess video skill more than content/knowledge
Screencast	Process; skill	Authentic (although editing may impact authenticity)	Time-intensive; requires some technical skill; may measure oral skill more than procedural skill
Oral presentation	Communicating knowledge	Authentic; flexible format (e.g., podcast)	May measure communication skills more than knowledge; time intensive
Bibliography	Process, comprehension	Authentic, cheap	Prone to plagiarism; time intensive; need to determine relative importance of citation process/ product and resources selected
Research report	Process (accessing, selecting, writing, organizing, etc.); comprehension	Authentic, nuanced; flexible formats	Assessment may be subjective; might assess writing or format-use skill more than content knowledge

Assessment Instrument	Measures	Advantages	Disadvantages
Demonstration	Process	Authentic	May be hard to grade; time intensive
Authentic performance (carry out task)	Process, comprehension, knowledge	Realistic, nuanced	May be hard to grade, especially if the task is complex; time intensive
Rubric	Process, product	Quick, easy, cheap, standardized, identifies criteria	Needs to be carefully developed in order to be valid (tension between generalizability and nuance)

What are the opportunities for the school librarian program to design instruction with the rest of the school community?

DESIGN

Designing instruction involves decisions about content, resources, learning activities, and the logistics for delivering the instructional design.

Content and Resources

The outcomes and objectives determine the content—the "what" of learning. School librarians then choose what resources are needed in order to teach the content. In classrooms, textbooks traditionally provided the basis for resources, but the library's collection—and access to digital resources—offers a spectrum of possible relevant information. The choice of resources also depends on their use.

- For independent comprehension: textual, visual, and multimedia materials
- For interactive learning: simulations, games, and interactive tutorials
- For socially constructed learning: social media
- For teaching: presentation slides and handouts
- For production: productivity suites (e.g., word processing, spreadsheets) and multimedia editors

The format of the resource also impacts the choice of resource, for example, video represents dynamic processes better than text and visual guides represent plants better than text-only resources.

Learning objects are increasingly popular resources to use. These self-contained resources may be integrated into the curriculum content as appropriate. Examples of learning objects include simulations, readings, presentations, tutorials, assessments, and so forth. A good list of learning-object repositories may be found at http://uiuc.libguides.com/content.php?pid=64638&sid=514221.

In choosing resources, school librarians should consider the learners' needs, such as language, reading level, learning-style preferences, ease of use, and accessibility. Technology introduces another set of criteria: site and remote access, equipment requirements, and technology skills. Furthermore, school librarians may need to allocate additional time to teach a technology skill so that students can use the technology to gain and demonstrate competence.

Occasionally, school librarians adapt or originate resources, particularly for handouts, because existing material needs synthesis, simplification, or local customization. Fair use usually covers the copyright issue if the adapted materials are being used for onsite education and research. The amount and substantiality of the material used should not impact the potential market or value of the copyrighted work. For copyright guidance, consult http://www.copyright.gov/title17/ and http://csulb.libguides.com/c.php?g=39326&p=250439.

Whenever they are creating resources, school librarians should follow these tips:

- Write clearly and unambiguously. Use simple sentence structure and vocabulary.
- Use visuals to clarify steps, such as screen "dumps."
- Number steps and provide sufficient white space between steps in order to ease readability.
- If there is a chance that the reader might make a mistake (as in following a procedure), explain how to correct the mistake and proceed.
- Provide a glossary of library terms as needed.
- Read text aloud in order to tell if it is clear, and have a target audience member (e.g., student) try using the documentation.

Learning Activities

Through learning activities, students can explore and practice information and digital literacies. As implied above, resources can be used to convey content and be manipulated by students to gain competence. Typically, students practice first under the supervision of the teacher and then hone their skills or apply the knowledge independently. It is also possible for students initially to engage in a learning activity by themselves and then generate questions for the instructor to answer and give guidance for deeper understanding.

Designing learning activities involves several factors. Objectives drive the content, and standards drive the assessment. How the activity enables students to meet those objectives drives the design specifics.

- *Space:* Where will the activity occur? In the classroom, the library, elsewhere, virtual?
- *Time frame:* How long will the activity last? Will it be done in one session or more? Will the activity be subdivided into smaller steps? Is timing strict or self-paced?
- *Personnel:* Who will instruct? The librarian, the classroom teacher, outside presenter, combination?
- *Teaching strategy:* How will the activity be introduced? Presentation, video, screencast, demonstration, case study, learning stations, game, hands-on exploration, digital tutorial, WebQuest?
- *Prerequisite skills:* Technology skill, procedural skills such as outlining, and so forth?
- *Affective domain:* What are ways to get the learners' attention? Type of motivation? Means of emotional engagement? Ways to incorporate social skills?
- *Grouping of learners:* Individual, small group, entire class?
- *Product or evidence:* What will the students do and produce? Discussion, debate, oral presentation, podcast? Report, white paper, content analysis, blog, poem? Spreadsheet, chart, infographic? Illustration, collage, graphic organizer, model? Skit, song, video?
- *Differentiation:* How will different students' learning preferences and needs be addressed? Choice of source material or means to demonstrate competence? Time differential? Extended activity or product? Assistive technology?
- *Context:* How does the learning activity fit within a course or larger community? How do learners make connections between the learning activity and their own lives?

These factors work hand in hand and need to align and reinforce each other. For instance, if students are learning procedural skills, then demonstration is an appropriate teaching strategy, and the activity itself should be hands-on, preferably in the environment in which learners will apply their skill. Table 5.2 suggests ways to align desired knowledge types, instructional strategies, and evidence of learning.

Because information and digital literacies are more likely to be learned and integrated when contextualized in content-rich experiences, school librarians strive to design instruction collaboratively with subject-matter class-

Table 5.2. Lesson Activity Alignment

Type of Knowledge	Instructional Strategies	Evidence of Learning
Declarative knowledge	Link prior knowledge to new knowledge (e.g., concept maps). Organize information (e.g., graphic organizers). Elaborate/give details about the new knowledge (e.g., analogies, imagery).	Accurate and detailed concept map; correct paper-and-pencil test answers
Conceptual knowledge	Provide definitions, examples, and counterexamples (e.g., "An apple is a fruit, a carrot is *not* a fruit. The difference is . . .").	Correct learner-generated example; concept map
Conceptual knowledge	Use a concept attainment model: provide matched examples and nonexamples; learners make hypotheses about the underlying concept.	Increasingly accurate student-generated hypotheses and examples
Procedural knowledge	Demonstrate the essential, simplest process, then point out the major decision points, going from the start to the end.	Process listed, traced, or performed accurately and thoroughly
Procedural knowledge	Divide a process into stages or phases. Demonstrate one stage and have learners practice it. Then demonstrate the next stage, and so on, until the entire process is covered.	Process listed, traced, or performed accurately and thoroughly
Problem solving	Simulate the problem. Principles may be presented at the beginning, with learners testing the principles via test cases (deductive learning), or learners may explore the simulation and figure out the principles (inductive learning).	Correctly solved problem with appropriate process
Problem solving	Present case studies and have learners respond to the situation as if they were the decision makers. Contributing factors and problem-solving strategies are then derived. Case studies are useful for "soft" skills and complex or ill-structured problems.	Well-justified, appropriate decision-making process and recommendation
Cognitive strategy	Provide an overview of the strategy's specific steps, model the strategy (and think aloud), and give examples/nonexamples of applying the strategy. Guide the learner through a practice cognitive strategy (e.g., researching a topic).	Accurate and thorough flow chart; final product and self-reflection; I-Search paper

Type of Knowledge	Instructional Strategies	Evidence of Learning
Attitude learning	Model desired behavior. Have learners role play desired behavior and process feelings, attitudes, behaviors, and consequences. Reinforce desired behavior.	Self-assessment and peer assessment; observation of behavior
Psychomotor skills	Model and have learners practice the skill progressively: step 1, then steps 1 and 2, then steps 1 and 2 and 3, etc.	Skill performance
Psychomotor skills	1. Explain the skill and the sequence of steps. 2. Model the skill and have learners physically practice the skill. 3. Coach learner practice until skills are done automatically and flawlessly.	1. Describe skill and list steps 2. Guided skill performance 3. Automatic skill performance

room teachers. Therefore, all of the above factors have to be negotiated between the two parties. As such, they will need to share control, which may be difficult for the classroom teacher. While the teacher can situate the learning activity within the context of a course, the librarian can also link the learning activity to the overall information and digital literacy repertoire of skills. More details about collaborative curriculum will be covered in the following chapter.

The following lesson plan template is one way to structure all of the above elements:

- Lesson Title:
- Grade Level:
- Subject:
- Lesson Overview:
- Time Frame:
- Learning Objectives: Learners will . . .
- Content Standards (aligned with Common Core):
- Information Standards (aligned with Common Core):
- Digital Literacy Standards (aligned with Common Core):
- Resources (note personnel, space, and materials):
- Prerequisite Skills:
- Planning for Diverse Learners:
- Instructional Strategies and Learning Activities:
- Variations:
- Assessment:

DEVELOPING THE CURRICULUM PACKAGE

The instructional design "package" consists of the entire learning session, including feedback, along with possible preplanning and follow-up details. Unless the session is a one-shot isolated event, which should not be the case in school settings, the learning session is part of an overall curriculum with content, standards, instruction, learning, and assessment. As such, the parts all have to fit together and be sequenced logically and developmentally for optimum learning.

That arrangement needs to consider the logical progression of concepts and skills. For instance, before students can effectively locate information, they need to know the concept of main ideas and key terms. Thus, making a KWL (what I know, what I want to know, what I learned) chart is a useful learning activity to do before teaching locational strategies. School librarians can create a flow chart or series of progression steps to sequence learning sessions over a period of time in order to create a learning unit. The above sequence reflects conceptual and skill-based development. Other ways to sequence learning activities include

- simple to complex (e.g., creating citations)
- concrete to abstract (e.g., text analysis)
- specific to general (e.g., research strategies)
- basic features to advanced features (e.g., presentation tools)
- procedural steps (e.g., video production)
- chronological

It should be noted that learning activities may also "branch," providing optional scaffolding or enrichment information. In that respect, a good approach is to design the basic content and learning activities and then provide links to alternative material.

The ultimate curriculum package typically includes the following features:

- Introduction to the overall curriculum, including content, learning objectives, and rationale for the curriculum
- Associated standards (e.g., academic subject matter, Common Core State Standards, information literacy, digital literacy)
- Introduction of the instructor(s) and students (e.g., brief profiles and icebreaker activities)
- Explanation of the curriculum structure: how to navigate the "package" and other logistics (e.g., how to retrieve resources)
- Expectations and responsibilities of the instructor(s) and learners: deadlines, feedback, etiquette, support

- Resource materials: to gain and demonstrate knowledge and skills
- Learning activities: description, rationale, directions, resources, support, differentiation
- Intended assessments: evidence/product, assessment instrument, standard, logistics
- Communication mechanisms
- Methods for building engagement and community
- Instructor information: needed preparation, tips, support materials

Some instructional packages can be self-contained and experienced by the student independent of the classroom. For instance, digital interactive tutorials can provide practice and give specific feedback based on the student's responses. Such tutorials need to be developed very carefully and thoroughly in order to address differences in learning and are usually better suited for declarative and procedural knowledge (e.g., locating research articles, such as http://www.uic.edu/depts/lib/reference/services/tutorials/Tutorial--Final%20Version.swf) if they are expected to be self-contained activities without "live" instructor follow-up.

Before the designed instruction and its package are implemented, they should be pilot tested. Ideally, both a peer, such as another school librarian or relevant classroom teacher, and a target student, such as a student who learned the content recently, should try out the curriculum package. If possible, the testers should orally discuss their process with either the librarian observing their actions or having the testing session videotaped for later analysis. The instructional designer can then interview the testers to get future input and make changes accordingly in order to provide the optimum learning experience for the target learners.

IMPLEMENTATION

The instructional design looks great. It has meaningful content and is thoroughly planned. Does it work? It takes real learners in a real learning environment to find out. Hopefully, the initial state of planning examined the learning environment and its constraints so that the instruction can be designed within a realistic context.

One obvious factor to consider in the implementation is that of the learning environment, which is typically established before the instruction begins. For instance, if instruction occurs in the library, the site's general atmosphere and behavioral expectations should already be in place. In anticipation of the actual instruction, the school librarian should make sure that the room arrangement and resources are set, including handouts and supplies.

Of course, instruction becomes alive when the students arrive. They should be greeted and guided to the learning area. Ideally, the school librarian should inform the classroom teacher ahead of time about seating and needed resources for the class to bring so that the students come focused and prepared to learn.

For optimum learning, the classroom teacher should accompany the class and remain for the instruction, even if he or she does not explicitly conduct the lesson, because the teacher is part of the learning community and the learning activity impacts classroom instruction. Moreover, the classroom teacher is likely to know the students better than the school librarian, so he or she can help monitor and manage the class's behavior. It is also helpful if the classroom teacher alerts the school librarian about possible student issues or specific needs (e.g., hearing impairment, recent parent loss).

Class management itself impacts the implementation effectiveness; in fact, class management significantly determines both the instructor's and students' success (Marzano, Marzano, & Pickering, 2003). Students learn best in a safe, caring, supportive, and intellectually stimulating environment. Since most school librarians have teaching experience, this aspect should not be a challenge, except when student behavior norms differ from the classroom. Again, the school librarian and classroom teacher should clarify behavior expectations ahead of time. In addition, well-planned instruction should optimize organizational and interactive aspects of learning. As noted earlier, having all of the resources and instructional aids in place ahead of time helps establish a positive learning environment. In any case, some tips for classroom management follow.

- Develop respectful relationships with all students, and treat everyone fairly.
- Communicate effectively, clearly, and articulately.
- Quickly gain students' attention, and engage them actively.
- State the learning objective and direction, and motivate students by linking the objective to personally meaningful contexts.
- Attend to both cognitive and affective domains of learning. Engage all of the senses.
- Tolerate different levels of participation if possible, but make sure that every student has the opportunity to participate actively.
- Reinforce positive behavior. Build on positive peer pressure.
- Check frequently for understanding, and clarify relevant questions along the way.
- Watch pacing. Can all of the students keep up? Is more time needed for explanation?

- Provide the essential concepts and directions for the learning activity, enough to get students started, and then scaffold smaller groups or individuals who are "stuck."
- Provide alternative or extension activities for students who meet the objective before the end of the session; alternatively, have such students serve as peer coaches for the remaining students.
- Be prepared for the unexpected; have a backup plan.

Collaborative learning activities require additional direction. At the least, students need to be grouped physically, which may involve moving and reseating. Typically, collaborative activities involve individual roles or responsibilities, so the school librarian needs to determine how those roles will be designated (e.g., by numbering off, disseminating role cards, having groups choose roles for each person, etc.). The school librarian also has to make sure that each student knows how to carry out his or her role before the activity begins. The school librarian has to clarify group processing, such as note taking, ensuring that all individuals participate and keeping the group on task and mindful of the time frame.

When instruction occurs in a computer lab or incorporates multiple laptops, additional management issues arise. As noted earlier, students need to know how to use the technology in order to access and learn the concepts. While students may be paired for a learning activity, with mixed technology abilities, both need to access and manipulate the equipment. As with other library behavior expectations, norms for technology use should be reviewed and procedures posted for easy reference. For example, unlike the print environment, the Internet environment is much more open ended, and students may veer off into nonrelevant areas. Fortunately, when students successfully find and engage with digital resources, they are likely to keep on track. Setting the computer screen to the desired source material through the library portal eases access and navigation; installing lab management software such as Fortres and Deep Freeze can also cut down on hacking and other nonproductive computer use. Additionally, technology sometimes does not work properly, which then distracts from learning. In that respect, school librarians should precheck all technology, including web links, before instruction starts. They might also consider having a student or adult aide available to help troubleshoot technical problems during the learning activity. To minimize calls for help, school librarians can set up a signal, such as a plastic cup or sign set on top of the computer or monitor, to indicate that assistance is needed.

Once the learning activity begins, no matter the grouping or mode of learning, the school librarian monitors and assesses student effort, largely through close observation and active listening. At this point, individualized scaffolding and interventions come into play. Are students engaged and on task? If not, the school librarian needs to find out why and address the issue. Such actions demonstrate care for the students and a desire for their success. Sometimes several students may express a problem, in which case the school librarian would do well to alert the whole class and provide the appropriate intervention, such as clarifying directions or showing students how to navigate a website.

Part of design implementation is metacognitive. School librarians should provide time for students to synthesize and self-reflect on their learning, ideally in the midst of their activity as well as at the end of the session. The school librarian should reiterate the learning objective and check with the class as to their progress in meeting that objective. Such reflection can be as easy as a quick-write or class oral report-out about what was learned and what the next steps will be. What went well, and what still needs clarification or other support? This refocusing exercise also informs the school librarian of possible changes or additions to the instruction that can be addressed afterward—for this class or for a future population.

It should be noted that implementing instruction may occur completely independently of the instructor physically. For instance, students may do a self-paced online tutorial at school or elsewhere during the school day or at some other time. As with face-to-face instruction, virtual instruction needs to include checks for understanding, such as quizzes with feedback and review or summary sections. Even with these built-in checks, students may still need help, be it technical or conceptual. Therefore, such digital instructional packages need to provide help pages and possible contact information. If several students are doing the same activity, the school librarian might set a wiki for peer interaction and assistance. Also, as with face-to-face instruction, students need to have the resources to access the instruction, such as an Internet-connected computer, so such conditions for learning need to be ascertained ahead of time; otherwise, assumptions may prove frustrating for both the learner and the instructor.

EVALUATION

As noted above, assessment and evaluation occur throughout the instructional design process. As reflective practitioners, school librarians should check the effectiveness of each step and make timely changes as needed. This iterative process enables improvements to be made prior to the learning experience so that students have the maximum chance of learning efficiently. Checks and changes along the way also decrease the possibility that student learning shortcomings are caused by the design; instead, school librarians can look at the immediate implementation phase in order to identify and address learning problems.

Nevertheless, summative evaluation offers an end-run opportunity to review the entire instructional design process and make changes for its next use. Therefore, not only should school librarians analyze the learners and instruction but also the learning experience and instructional design itself. To that end, taking time to debrief right after the learning session maximizes the chances that future instructional design will be effective.

The most obvious evaluation consideration is student performance, which can be measured through examination of student products, actions, and attitudes. Certainly, school librarians want to know what factors contributed to student success—as well as factors that impeded success. I-Search papers constitute a wonderful opportunity to measure both process and product because students journal their efforts as they conduct personal research. A quick-write session can also serve as a way for students to self-reflect on their efforts and may provide useful input about ways to improve the instructional design. Another useful practice is peer review, both at the draft and final product stage, so that students can learn how well they communicate and also share advice about ways to improve their work.

At the same time, school librarians should evaluate the conditions in which the instruction and learning occur. Was the time frame appropriate? Was the physical space conducive for learning? Were the resources appropriate and readily available? Did all of the students have the support needed to succeed, such as having assistive technology or scaffolding? Did factors outside of the school librarian's control, such as emergencies or power outages, impact student learning?

The instructors themselves need to self-reflect on their efforts. What went well, and what could be improved? How well prepared were they? How well did they implement the instructional design? Was time used efficiently? How well did they engage learners and interact with them? How well did they manage the learning environment?

Instruction that is designed collaboratively adds another dimension of evaluation. How well did collaborators communicate, plan, and work together? How effective was the allocation of responsibilities and workload? To what extent did each person interact and build on each other's contributions, modifying efforts as needed?

The ultimate question remains: How did the instructional design impact student learning?

INSTRUCTIONAL DESIGN ISSUES

Instructional design needs to consider content, learners, instructors, and the learning environment. As such, a one-size-fits-all approach seldom results in optimum learning. Some representative issues are addressed here.

Technology-Enhanced Instructional Design

Mishra and Koehler's (2006) TPACK (technological pedagogical content knowledge; see figure 5.1) framework represents the knowledge that instructors need in order to teach effectively with technology. As it applies to school librarians teaching information literacy, the model notes the following knowledge bases:

- Content knowledge (CK): information and digital literacy
- Pedagogical knowledge (PK): general principles and practices of teaching and learning
- Technology knowledge (TK): digital literacy
- Pedagogical content knowledge (PCK): how to teach information and digital literacy (e.g., inquiry-based teaching)
- Technological content knowledge (TCK): technology related to information and digital literacy (e.g., online databases, integrated library management systems)
- Technological pedagogical knowledge (TPK): knowledge of technologies that can facilitate teaching and learning (e.g., videos, simulations, online collaborative tools)
- Technological Pedagogical Content Knowledge (TPACK): the intersection of the knowledge bases, such as technology-enhanced instruction and learning of information and digital literacy

As mentioned before, technology impacts teaching and learning and certainly should be considered during instructional design. School librarians may well teach *about* technology, such as creating spreadsheets, as much as teaching *with* technology, such as having students use spreadsheets in order to make predications. Furthermore, school librarians realize that interacting with technology does not guarantee learning. Generally, technology integration is beneficial when accessing digital resources, providing multisensory experiences, offering repetitive rote practice, supporting offsite learning, and recording or archiving communication. Technology is less effective for face-to-face personal contact and use of in-house, nontechnical resources.

School librarians should also consider student learning preferences when deciding about technology incorporation; technology can motivate some students, scaffold English learners because of translation tools, and support self-directed learning. On the other hand, some students are uncomfortable with technology or prefer nonmediated learning with technology. When in doubt, school librarians should use the most stable, low-tech solution, if for no other reason than because of physical and intellectual access to technologies. Whenever technology is incorporated, school librarians need to assess students' current status relative to technology availability and skills and build in

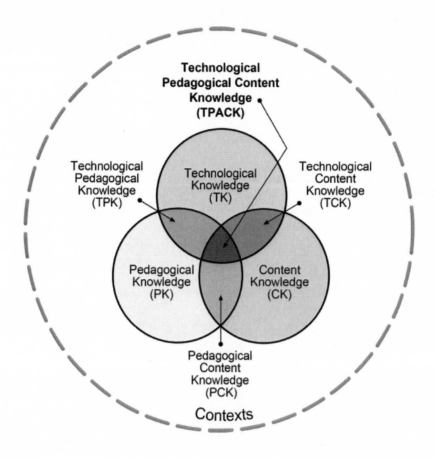

Figure 5.1. **TPACK.** *Reproduced by permission of the publisher, © 2012 by tpack.org*

added time to address those prerequisite skills. Furthermore, as noted above, technology doesn't always work, so school librarians need to have a plan B or at the least troubleshoot the problem and figure out a solution or work-around.

Universal Design for Learning

Learners vary widely in terms of background, experience, physical differences, languages, interests, personalities, and values. Therefore, instructional design needs to provide choices for ways that learners can access and engage with the curriculum and express themselves and take action. For instance, information should be represented in multiple formats and levels of complexity. A concept might be represented by words and images with a means to read the text aloud.

Here are some more specific tips for designing inclusive learning experiences:

- Provide a safe, positive, and caring learning environment. Encourage intellectual risk taking.
- Structure instruction clearly and explicitly.
- Use simple vocabulary and sentence structure. Paraphrase, repeat, and summarize frequently.
- Provide specialized content matter glossaries.
- Use visual aids and graphic organizers.
- Provide ways to make learning meaningful for learners; help them connect content with their own lives and design authentic learning tasks.
- Provide concrete examples and applications as well as showing "the big picture."
- Provide individual and group learning activities.
- Emphasize both process and product; recognize and support efforts toward competency.
- Address cognitive and affective aspects of learning.
- Provide timely, specific feedback and give learners a chance to improve their effort and results. Check frequently for understanding.
- Scaffold learning as needed (e.g., break down or simplify tasks; provide additional resources; incorporate assistive technology; change time limits; use graphic organizers, provide peer coaches, or study buddies).
- And, of course, get to know learners individually.

Cultural Issues

Cultural differences impact instructional design as different groups vary in their experiences, norms, and values. Domer and Gorman (2006) identified five cultural dimensions that should be considered when designing instruction:

- *Student–teacher relations:* Some cultures reinforce a high power-distance relationship where the teacher is considered all knowing and not to be questioned; teachers may tend to lecture. In other cultures, such relationships are more egalitarian; constructivist learning supports this philosophy. School librarians should explicitly tell students how to address them (e.g., Mr. Alvaro, Ms. Librarian) and explain class expectations.
- *Learner participation:* Some cultures favor independent work, while others encourage group effort. Similarly, different cultures have conflicting views about competition and collaboration. School librarians should ex-

plain the norms of class participation (e.g., hands up to volunteer information, guidelines for teamwork, expected level of engagement) and design opportunities for learners to experience different modes of learning.

- *Topics of discussion:* Some topics may be taboo to discuss in public, such as birth control or family income. Typically, the classroom teacher has addressed these sensitivities already. In general, one-to-one conversation outside of earshot is practiced by librarians as a courtesy to all; alternatively, private e-mail or texting might be a way to handle sensitive topics discretely.
- *Choice of resources:* Fortunately, school librarians strive for balanced collections in various formats and reading levels. Librarians also try to avoid materials that are stereotypical or disrespectful. School librarians strive to help students learn how to evaluate sources critically, being mindful of cultural differences. It should be noted that in some cultures, students are not expected to choose or question sources, so this experience may be new and potentially uncomfortable for them.
- *Learning activities:* Similarly to choosing resources, choosing how to do an information task may feel uncomfortable for students from some cultures, so school librarians may have to guide these learners in such decision-making processes. For those students who are accustomed to rote learning, inquiry-based instruction may also seem strange; school librarians can provide question prompts or project structures to jumpstart thinking.

As a rule, declarative and procedural knowledge is less prone to cultural vagaries; the "softer" skills are more likely to be culturally defined and so need to be contextualized carefully. Older students might share their cultural perspectives and resources as active instructional design participants.

IMPLICATIONS FOR SCHOOL LIBRARIANS

Instructional design draws on school librarians' expertise in information processing and organization, incorporation of technology, selection of appropriate resources, teaching strategies, and information behavior. Furthermore, school librarians work with all students across all curricular areas, so they know what is developmentally appropriate and can help students transfer learning from one academic domain to another. These skills and broad knowledge can help school librarians advance their case to codesign instruction with classroom teachers and reinforce their ability to design instruction independently as part of the overall curricular picture, which is detailed in the next chapter.

REFERENCES

Association for Childhood Education International. (2007). *Elementary education standards and supporting explanation.* Washington, DC: Association for Childhood Education International.

Branson, R., & Rayner, G. (1975). *Interservice procedures for instructional systems development.* Tallahassee: Center for Educational Technology, Florida State University.

Domer, D., & Gorman, G. (2006). Information literacy education in Asian developing countries: Cultural factors affecting curriculum development and programme delivery. *IFLA Journal, 32*(4), 281–293.

Hubbell, E. (2010). Using McREL's knowledge taxonomy for ed tech professional development. *Learning & Leading with Technology, 37*(8), 20–23.

Marzano, R., Marzano, J., & Pickering, D. (2003). *Classroom management that works.* Alexandria, VA: Association of Supervision and Curriculum Development.

Mishra, P., & Koehler, M. (2006). Technological pedagogical content knowledge: A framework for teacher knowledge. *Teachers College Record, 108*(6), 1017–1054.

National Council for Accreditation of Teacher Education. (2008). *Unit standards in effect.* Washington, DC: National Council for Accreditation of Teacher Education.

Smaldino, S., & Lowther, D. (2011). *Instructional technology and media for learning* (10th ed.). Upper Saddle River, NJ: Pearson.

Chapter Six

Connecting the Curriculum

Just as with other curricula, an information and digital literacies curriculum has greater impact when aligned and interwoven throughout the school's curriculum. Yet probably the greatest challenge for school librarians is staking the claim of information and digital curriculum within the school. This chapter describes how to develop a scope-and-sequenced curriculum, keeping in mind the Common Core State Standards (CCSS) and other school curricula, including cocurricula. This kind of approach to the curriculum requires whole-school involvement of curriculum mapping as well as teaching interdependence.

Even more widely, the information and digital literacies curriculum should articulate between each level: from elementary to middle school, from middle school to high school, and even to postsecondary education. Especially as students need to be college and career ready, they need to develop lifelong skills and dispositions early on.

Schools also need to provide the conditions to support information and digital curricula. For example, administrators have to ensure that technology infrastructure can support the curriculum. These preconditions are often outside the control of school librarians, although they can influence decision makers.

This chapter provides strategies on ways for librarians to serve as bridges to their own site's faculty so that the curriculum will be widely and deeply integrated.

CURRICULUM CHARACTERISTICS

As noted in earlier chapters, a curriculum involves a systematic sequence of content, which includes instruction and learning activities so that students have opportunities to learn and practice the content matter. Elements of an information and digital literacies curriculum have already been discussed, especially in terms of standards. However, how that curriculum is detailed and implemented is more problematic. Few states and districts have developed a scope-and-sequence curriculum for information and digital literacies, although the CCSS have provided some structure for this task. Furthermore, curricular decisions ultimately land on the principal's desk, so school librarians must negotiate the curriculum with the rest of the school community, both in terms of its delivery and its preconditions.

The Association of College and Research Libraries (ACRL, 2012) developed characteristics of effective information literacy programs, which can be applied well to K–12 information and digital literacies curricula. Each factor involves collaboration with the school community; even a stand-alone curriculum needs community-wide buy-in to be accepted and implemented effectively.

- *Mission:* The curriculum should align with the school library's mission, which, in turn, should align with the school's and district's mission. The curriculum should also align with recognized information and digital literacies standards, as well as other school content standards. Additionally, the curriculum needs to be developed in collaboration with relevant stakeholders who agree with the mission.
- *Goals and Objectives:* The curriculum has measurable outcomes both in terms of student learning and curriculum assessment. The curriculum serves all students and accommodates the developmental and diverse needs of students.
- *Planning:* Curriculum planning addresses the findings of environmental scans, including school community support. The curriculum is tied to library and school planning and budget cycles. Planning prioritizes fiscal, material, and human resource allocation in collaboration with the school community. Planning includes a program of development for the library staff and the school community. A time line is established for curriculum review and improvement.
- *Administrative and institutional support:* Administrators delegate curriculum leadership and responsibility to school librarians and other relevant teachers. Administrators incorporate the curriculum into the school's mission, plan, policies, and procedures. Administrators allocate sufficient resources for the curriculum's effective implementation. Administrators communicate their support of the curriculum. Administrators encourage and reward curriculum collaboration and achievement.
- *Articulation:* The curriculum has a scope and sequence of content with associated student competencies. The curriculum is formalized, approved, and broadly disseminated. The curriculum emphasizes student-centered

learning and supports lifelong learning. The curriculum is integrated into the school's academic program.

- *Collaboration:* The curriculum is supported by the school community. The curriculum fosters cross-curricular discussion, planning, implementation, and assessment. The curriculum aligns information and digital literacies with disciplinary content.
- *Pedagogy:* The curriculum supports diverse teaching and learning approaches appropriate to the content. Pedagogy incorporates relevant technology. Pedagogy builds on learners' existing knowledge and skills, interests, and goals. Pedagogy promotes inquiry, active learning experiences, critical thinking, reflection, and recursive learning. Pedagogy contextualizes content in terms of other curricula. Pedagogy prepares students for lifelong learning.
- *Staffing:* Staffing is adequate to support the curriculum. The curriculum involves the collaboration of library staff, classroom teachers, other educational support staff, and administrators. School librarians have knowledge and experience in pedagogy, curriculum development and instructional design, and assessment. School librarians model lifelong learning and participate in professional development. School librarians are regularly evaluated and improve their practice.
- *Outreach:* School librarians clearly describe, communicate, and market the curriculum and its value to targeted audiences within the school community and to the community at large. School librarians share information about the curriculum and its implementation with the school community and beyond. School librarians conduct professional development sessions about the curriculum for the school community.
- *Assessment and evaluation:* School librarians develop and implement a process for curriculum planning, evaluation, and improvement. School librarians measure the extent to which the curriculum meets goals and objectives, including student learning, using appropriate data and assessment tools. Learning is assessed in terms of process and product. Assessments are diagnostic, formative, and summative. Findings are analyzed, and interventions are identified to improve the curriculum and student learning. School librarians integrate curriculum and student-learning assessment with other site and professional assessment and accreditation efforts.

SCOPE AND SEQUENCE

Existing information and digital literacies standards provide the framework for the curriculum, and the accompanying and developmental indicators guide the curriculum's scope and sequence. However, determining the actual curriculum can be challenging. For instance, a case can be made to separate information literacy from digital literacy in that the latter is likely to include technology operations (e.g., software installation, hardware troubleshooting, and learning productivity tools), which skilled librarians practice but seldom explicitly teach. However, the use of technology tools to access and use information in various formats does reflect information literacy and fits comfortably within librarians' instructional "portfolio." In any case, librarians should work with the rest of the school community in order to determine where those necessary technical skills should be taught.

This situation highlights the issue of scope in that information literacy might be considered the purview of every classroom teacher. Traditionally, information literacy is often linked with language arts, largely because of reading and writing. However, these processes occur in every course. Skills such as numerical analysis and visual representation of knowledge fall not only within the domains of mathematics and art but also exist within information literacy.

Even if the result is a stand-alone curriculum, parallel to other subject matter such as social studies or science, most school librarians would agree that the curriculum needs to be contextualized in order to make learning meaningful. In effect, school librarians teach students information and digital literacies in order to facilitate lifelong learning.

Curriculum Mapping

To that end, curriculum mapping offers a viable way to build the information and digital literacies curriculum. School librarians should lead this effort with administrative support and participation by the entire faculty. Were the school librarian to develop such a curriculum map alone, implementation would not occur. However, the school librarian might share existing information literacy standards and sample curricula with school leaders as a way to start a curricular discussion. For instance, in its follow-up publication *Standards for the 21st-Century Learner in Action*, the American Association of School Librarians (AASL, 2009) provides grade-specific indicators of information literacy and sample lessons. Then together the school's educators can identify the specific content and learning outcomes and the design instruction to support those outcomes. Logistically, a steering group of stakeholders, such as department or grade chairs, can liaise with their respective constituents so that rich conversation within each group can be reported out to the steering committee in order to facilitate the curriculum process. Ultimately, though, the entire faculty should weigh in on—and engage with—the curriculum.

In mapping the curriculum, each grade or department reviews the information and digital literacies outcomes and identifies their own learning activities that address the outcome. Reviews should also indicate whether they teach that content or assume students' ability to apply that knowledge or skill to their learning activity. For instance, students might be asked to create a digital story about an immigrant's journey to the United States. Such a project entails the information literacy research skills and digital storytelling skills. Are those skills taught at that point or are they assumed (or reviewed)? If taught, who provides that instruction? By mapping existing practice to the draft information and digital literacies outcomes, the steering committee can uncover gaps in teaching and learning, as well as gaps in the literacy outcomes.

The result is a reality-based information and digital literacies curriculum that spans academic domains and fosters coteaching and curriculum interdependence. For instance, if students learn how to locate ecology articles in online databases in their ninth-grade science class, they can apply that skill to research a social issue in their ninth-grade health education class. With that knowledge, classroom teachers can also work with school librarians to embed information literacy instruction, such as the use of atlases, into the classroom when that skill is needed to comprehend social studies concepts, as an example.

Table 6.1 curriculum map exemplifies this process, which results in an information and digital literacies curriculum scope and sequence.

Table 6.1. Curriculum Map

	Information & Digital Outcomes	Middle School	9th Grade	10th Grade	11th Grade	12th Grade
PROCESS	**SKILL**					
PLAN						
	Define task	x	English			
	Develop thesis/question/hypothesis	x	English	Science	Social Studies	
	Identify data needed			Science		
	Define role within group	x	Physical Education			
ACCESS						
	Identify "universe" of data		Social Studies			
	Use library facility	x				
	Use library portal	x				
	Use search/keywords	x				
	Use search engines and directories	x				
	Use online databases		Social Studies			
	Use social media		English			
	Use ready reference books	x				

Digital Outcomes

EVALUATE

Outcome						
Use data collection tools				Science		
Interview			Social Studies			
Identify main ideas	x					
Compare sources on same topic	x					
Identify point of view/fact vs. opinion	x					
Apply visual literacy		Arts				
Interpret graphs		Math	Math	Science		
Analyze numerical data			Math			
Analyze text		English	English	English	English	
Identify primary and secondary sources	x	Social Studies				
Determine quality of information		Social Studies	Social Studies	Social Studies		Social Studies
Use rubrics	x					
Evaluate research process			Science	Science	Social Studies	
Evaluate research product			Science	Science		Social Studies

Information & Digital Outcomes	Middle School	9th Grade	10th Grade	11th Grade	12th Grade
USE/APPLY					
Take notes	x				
Summarize	x				
Classify					
Sequence	x				
Use graphic organizer	x				
Outline	x				
Visualize info		Arts			
Manage sources		Social Studies			
Cite		Social Studies			
Avoid plagiarism	x				
COMMUNICATE PRODUCE					
Choose appropriate format to communicate information		Social Studies			
Produce bibliography	x				
Produce annotated bibliography		Social Studies			
Write critical review		English	English	English	English
Produce research paper			Science	Social Studies	

Information & Digital Outcomes	Middle School	9th Grade	10th Grade	11th Grade	12th Grade
Create visual product	x	Arts			
Present orally		English	English	English	English
Demonstrate		Science			
Create skit/play		Arts			
Author digital presentation		English			
Create video			Social Studies		
Create audio product		Social Studies			
Create web page					English
Create social media product				English	

It should be noted that the curriculum map should incorporate only required courses if the idea is to ensure that all students learn, practice, and demonstrate competency. At the very least, instruction in information and digital literacies needs to occur in required courses; practice and refinement can occur in electives such as world languages and in cocurricular offerings such as debate clubs and drama productions.

The CCSS also drive the curriculum, and many schools have mapped the standards to their existing curriculum. Fortunately, information and digital literacies are found throughout CCSS, as mentioned in earlier chapters; so if schools have done their CCSS mapping, they can easily find any remaining information and digital literacies gaps. Typically, basic procedures are likely to be subsumed in the broader CCSS and so are not explicitly stated, such as computer operations (e.g., saving files, navigating the Internet) and keyword Boolean searching.

College/Career Readiness

Increasingly, the community at large is calling for K–12 schools to make sure that their graduates are prepared for postsecondary futures, be they education or immediate career. Businesses want entering employees to demonstrate effective skills in reading, communication, technology, collaboration, and problem solving; academia has the same expectations for entering students. Currently, these same entities assert that many high school graduates do not have these skills. For instance, many higher education faculty complain about students' poor writing and research skills, and their librarians state that students have difficulty finding and evaluating scholarly materials. The need for information literacy, including the ability to learn independently, is apparent.

By analyzing these postsecondary needs, school librarians can determine what information literacy concepts and skills should be explicitly taught. Fortunately, the path between K–12 and higher education has been laid to some extent. Oakleaf and Owen (2010) examined the AASL K–12 learning standards and noted how those standards are transferrable to tasks that students do in college as they work with articles, reference materials, and data. Furthermore, the ACRL information literacy framework was informed by AASL's efforts. This task, however, is problematic in schools without librarians or in schools where those librarians are not at the curriculum table. Furthermore, such instruction needs to occur throughout Grades K–12, not just in high school. Just as mathematics builds upon prior learning, so do information and digital literacies.

Articulation

Because information literacy undergirds lifelong learning, school librarians and other educators should also think about articulating information literacy curriculum between school levels, such as elementary to middle school, middle school to high school, and high school to local postsecondary institutions. By providing a seamless information and digital literacies curriculum, educators can build on prior experiences and optimize learning. Table 6.1, for instance, notes those outcomes that are expected to be met upon graduation from middle school.

Especially as policy makers are pushing career and college readiness, the need for articulated information literacy curricula becomes even more apparent. Technically, these literacy outcomes should be met, at least at a basic level, by the time that the student finishes his or her sophomore year of high school because junior college courses and technical courses may be educational options for students. In such cases, junior and senior high school students can focus on applying their literacies in light of specific disciplines, such as drama or history.

Such articulation demands that librarians build relationship across educational borders. For instance, middle school librarians can work with their feeder elementary school librarians in order to make sure that students from various sites have a level playing field when they enter middle school. In the process, elementary school librarians can compare their information and digital literacies curricula and share beneficial practices that support all students. Librarians can also share student assignment and sample work, which provides authentic evidence of developmentally appropriate learning activities. In some cases, librarians may discover that students in earlier grades have similar assignments at higher grades, and the products may also reflect more advanced knowledge than was assumed.

Likewise, local postsecondary librarians can inform high school librarians about their institutions' information and digital literacies expectations of entering students. Ideally, special librarians in local companies can share their employers' information and digital literacies standards for entry-level positions, which then enables high school librarians to share those expectations with other teachers and reinforces the need for the information and digital literacies curriculum.

COLLABORATION

As noted in the mapping discussion above, collaboration is key in incorporating information and digital literacies into the curriculum. If the school decides to offer stand-alone information and digital literacies courses, then those courses have to be approved by site and district governance and probably by the state. If information and digital literacies are woven into the "fabric" of existing academic courses, it needs to be done systematically so that all students have opportunities to gain competence. Such systematic work is most likely to be done in collaboration with the school librarian, who has deep knowledge about information and digital literacies. The school librarian cannot teach information and digital literacies effectively without the support of the school community. While classroom teachers are the main instructional partners, librarians can also collaborate with specialists (e.g., tech experts, reading specialists), other support staff (e.g., health professionals, counselors), cocurricular supervisors (e.g., athletic directors, activity advisors), and administrators.

Under that broad umbrella of information and digital literacies, exist different forms of collaboration over time and different degrees of working together. Montiel-Overall (2005) identified four levels of interaction:

- *Networking*: information social interactions that can lead to joint efforts. For instance, the librarian might talk about a concept-mapping tool during faculty lunchtime.
- *Cooperation*: a give-and-take working relationship that helps each party further its goals. For instance, a librarian might prepare a bibliography of websites for a teacher who has the class researching ecology issues.
- *Coordination*: a formal relationship between equal partners. For instance, the teacher might reserve the library's computer lab for students to create wikis about their research.
- *Collaboration*: an interdependent working relationship involving a shared vision, planning, development, implementation, and assessment. Collaboration involves both social and intellectual interaction. For instance, the librarian and teacher might develop an I-Search unit.

These different kinds of interactions vary among individuals and can change over a career span. Even within one course, interactions can differ depending on the content and the learning activity at any given time. For instance, librarians might not work with math teachers when quadratic equations are being taught, but they could share recreational math games with students in a cooperative role or help students research mathematicians collaboratively based on coplanning and coteaching. As a general practice, librarians should strive for effective long-term working relationships that can adapt to momentary needs.

Finding the time to interact, especially to collaborate, can prove challenging. While some schools schedule joint planning time, many other schools relegate interaction to faculty meeting time, which can be filled with announcements and other one-way communication. Fortunately, with the advent of social media, collaborative tools have greatly expanded. Some are

less interactive, such as blogs, and others tend to promote informal cooperation rather than collaboration, such as Pinterest and Instagram. Google tools
such as Docs, Drive, and Hangouts are probably the most popular means to
collaborate substantially.

Another aspect of collaboration that is sometimes underrecognized is assessment. Too often school librarians help students get started on research
projects but never get to see the end results. At the very least, librarians
should ask teachers to see representative student work (such as sample A, B,
C grades and low-achieving product) in order to talk about successful aspects
and areas for instructional improvement. Librarians can also participate in
class debriefing discussions about students' efforts and obstacles in order to
identify resource and service needs. This conversation can be done virtually
using online conferencing tools if the librarian needs to stay in the library.
Librarians also need to assess the collaborative efforts themselves: planning,
use of resources, and instruction.

- How effective was the communication?
- How well were differences of opinion managed?
- Were responsibilities allocated effectively?
- How well was the plan carried out?
- How effective was each person?
- What changes need to be made in terms of the plan?
- What will be the nature of the collaboration in the future?

Taking the time to assess collaborative efforts facilitates improvement of
both the curriculum and collaboration.

INFRASTRUCTURE

Curriculum is situated within the working of the school and district. Its
successful implementation depends on the school's mission, organizational
structure, and culture, as well as its allocation of resources and services.
School librarians need to identify and work with these contextual conditions
in order to optimize efforts to help students become informationally and
digitally competent.

Facilities can drive curriculum in that they largely determine what kind of
instruction will occur and what physical resources are available to use—not
only informational sources but also the equipment that might be needed to
access nonprint and digital materials. Is there sufficient seating and working
surfaces for one or more classes? Is space available for formal presentations,
including darkened areas for projections? Are outlets and Internet connectiv-

ity handy? Is there production space for students to create multimedia products?

Virtual space complements physical space and can serve as an effective learning environment. Does the library have access to a secure server? Does the library have a portal for offering information and digital curriculum learning materials and activities such as learning objects? Can the school community access this portal remotely?

Time is needed for both planning and instruction. The school's daily schedule frames learning activities in that block scheduling facilitates substantive research projects. Are students expected to have a class every period, which may impact individual use of the library? While flexible schedules are a marker of high school programs, middle school libraries may mix fixed and flexible scheduling, which impacts planning. As noted before, school schedules vary in terms of preparation and planning time for both classroom teachers and school librarians, and joint time may be at a premium, especially for department- or grade-wide collaboration.

Curriculum practices impact information and digital literacies integration. How are courses developed: by individuals, site committees, or district committees? How are courses reviewed and approved? What role does the library play? How are courses related to each other? Are cross-disciplinary and multidisciplinary courses or units supported? Does the administration support coplanning or coteaching? What cocurriculars are offered?

Resources for teaching and learning often reflect educational philosophies. For instance, some schools base the curriculum on standardized textbooks and pacing guides. Some subject departments supplement textbooks with prescribed readings, which may include primary sources. Some courses include research assignments, which may consist of synthesizing informational texts, while other research projects might involve generating knowledge. Resources can be very expensive, so how the school governance allocates resources for classroom teaching and libraries often reveals the school's comparative value of different types of learning.

Technology increasingly requires significant funding—of equipment, servers, software, digital resources, online subscriptions, wi-fi and other Internet connectivity means, and other telecommunication costs. Additionally, the effective use of technology also requires specialists for academic and administrative technology access and maintenance. To what extent is the library supported? Technology integration also depends on the school community's attitudes and knowledge about it. How do administrators support technology integration through resource allocation, curricular expectations, professional development, and technical support?

School culture itself impacts how information and digital literacies are integrated. To what degree are academics valued by administrators, teachers, parents, and students? What are the school's measures of success? How open minded are decision makers? Who are the decision makers, and how do they make decisions? How are policies and procedures developed and reinforced? Is continuous improvement the norm, or is the status quo more highly valued? Do communities of practice exist? Is there an atmosphere of collaboration and teamwork, or do most people act independently? What are the typical teaching methods: lecture- or inquiry-based? Is independent or collaborative learning preferred? Are students grouped heterogeneously or tracked? Does the school have a culture of reading? What are the attitudes and practices around technology?

Parents and other community members also have a voice in how information and digital literacies are supported. What are their own literacy competencies and practices? What literacy hopes and expectations do they have for their children? Do they have access to reading materials and technology? How involved are they in school matters, including the support of the library? How does the school administration—and the librarian—interact and support parent engagement?

School librarians should conduct an environmental scan of their school, and perhaps their district, in order to determine the status of each of the above factors. What is the impact, positive and negative, of each factor? Which factors can the librarian leverage or influence? What role can the librarian play relative to each factor? Who can help the librarian as an advocate to ensure that the school's infrastructure, both physical and social, supports the information and digital literacies curriculum? What human relationships, particularly with influential persons, does the librarian need to establish and nurture? In the process, librarians also need to identify what resources and expertise they bring to the table to advance information and literacy curriculum, and they need to make their case convincingly. Only then will the school community understand the importance of information and digital literacies and provide the infrastructure for its curricular integration.

MIDDLE SCHOOL TEACHER WORKSHOP:
LEARNING ABOUT TECHNOLOGY

4:00 p.m.–4:05 p.m.	*Introductions and overview*
4:05 p.m.–4:20 p.m.	*Tech in the world* Tech in education: http://www.vimeo.com/ 4676849 Teachers watch video clips about technology careers

http://www.pbskids.org/designsquad/
     parentseducators/resources/
http://www.sciencekids.co.nz/sciencefacts/
     engineering/typesofengineeringjobs.html

Debrief about jobs

4:20 p.m.–4:30 p.m.   *Tech standards: ISTE and ITEEA*

https://www.iste.org/standards/standards-for-
     students
http://www.iteea.org

Teachers compare the two standards
Teachers view standards' resources
Show http://ca.mousesquad.org/educators/
     resources/
Teachers brainstorm ways that they can integrate
     standards

4:30 p.m.–4:45 p.m.   *How computers work*
Teachers watch video and explore resources

http://www.gcflearnfree.org/
     COMPUTERBASICS
http://www.abcya.com/computer_vocabulary.
     htm—to explore
Show http://www.commoncraft.com

4:45 p.m.–5:00 p.m.   *Coding*
Show http://www.infinitethinking.org/itm-35---
     coding-to-learn.html
Teachers explore coding training program:

http://www.crunchzilla.com/code-monster

5:00 p.m.–5:15 p.m.   *Design process*
Show http://pbskids.org/designsquad/
     parentseducators/workshop/process.html
Teachers see design process and trace it in video
     examples

http://k12videos.mit.edu/content/the-three-
     little-pigs-build-by-the-river
http://www.teachengineering.org/editors_
     choice.php

	Teachers brainstorm ways that they can integrate standards
5:15 p.m.–5:25 p.m.	*Connecting with families in learning about technology*
	http://cyberfamilies.blogspot.com http://k12digitalcitizenship.wikispaces.com Note: http://pbskids.org/designsquad/ parentseducators/
5:25 p.m.–5:30 p.m.	*Teachers share learning and identify next steps*

IMPLICATIONS FOR SCHOOL LIBRARIANS

Integrating the information and digital curriculum into the school's practice requires extensive expertise, preparation, planning, collaboration, and advocacy. School librarians need to know the lay of the land: the curriculum, the school's organization and culture, and the resources, both physical and human, in order to make such a curriculum successful. It is hard work and requires leader support as well as school community buy-in.

Even the best information and digital literacies curriculum has to be marketed effectively because the school community is likely to be unaware of the benefits of such a curriculum. School librarians need to interest decision makers and show how an information and digital literacies curriculum can address their needs, largely couched in terms of student success. Certainly, a literature review can point out how such a curriculum has contributed to student learning and college/career readiness in other locales. Librarians also have to gather and analyze relevant data once the curriculum is implemented in order to prove its effectiveness. The benefits of such long-term work? Increasing student literacy and success, supported by an effective library program.

REFERENCES

American Association of School Librarians. (2009). *Standards for the 21st century learner in action*. Chicago, IL: American Library Association.

Association of College and Research Libraries. (2012). *Characteristics of programs of information literacy that illustrate best practices*. Chicago, IL: American Library Association.

Montiel-Overall, P. (2005). A theoretical understanding of TLC. *School Libraries Worldwide, 11*(2), 24–48.

Oakleaf, M., & Owen, P. (2010). Closing the 12–13 gap together: School and college librarians supporting 21st century learners. *Teacher Librarian, 37*(4), 52–58.

Chapter Seven

Model Curriculum for Middle School

This chapter provides a scope-and-sequence curriculum for Grades 6–8. It offers a model stand-alone course with sample modules/units and learning activities. It also suggests different configurations for delivering a curriculum and notes how modules can be incorporated into an existing academic curriculum.

CONTENT

Information literacy encompasses several performance indicators for middle schoolers:

- *Planning:* articulating information needs and tasks, research question, hypothesis, thesis statement
- *Accessing information:* search engines and directories, library catalogs, subject headings and keywords, indexes, bibliographies, surveys, interviews, science probes and other peripherals
- *Evaluation:* of websites and other resources, main ideas and supporting evidence, point of view and bias, comparing primary and secondary sources, comparing resources, information representation (textual, visual, aural)
- *Manipulation:* note taking and other information extraction methods, identifying patterns and trends, organizing, synthesizing, making inferences and conclusions with supporting evidence, chart and graph, spreadsheet, database, calculator, computer-aided design (CAD), simulations
- *Communication:* matching communication channel with content and audience, publishing, presentation tools, graphic organizer, visual tools, ani-

mation, video, podcast, web page, social media, model, oral presentation, telecommunications, attribution (i.e., citation), collaborating

Likewise, digital literacy encompasses several performance indicators for middle schoolers:

- *Technology operations:* installation of software and apps, use of computer peripherals, use of computers and portable digital devices (e.g., access, storage, output, management, troubleshooting)
- *Use of productivity tools:* word processing (formatting, spell/grammar check, inserting media, document information), spreadsheet (formatting, formulas, graphs), database (fields, sorting), presentations (formatting, inserting media)
- *Use of visual tools:* paint and draw tools, graphic organizers, animation, cameras, camcorders
- *Use of the Internet:* navigation, search engines and directories, databases (and aggregators), evaluation of information, transfer of information, social media, online collaboration
- *Digital citizenship:* keeping safe, ethical and legal behavior, civic engagement

SAMPLE LEARNING ACTIVITIES

Middle school is the prime time to do inquiry-based projects. The curriculum often has multidisciplinary units, and students are usually literate enough to be able to read subject-specific materials as well as communicate in several ways. Information and digital literacies can be melded together in authentic projects that stress investigative processes. Here is one learning activity example.

Learning Activity: Budgeting for Now and the Future

Overview: In today's society, money management can be challenging. Middle schoolers can proactively think about how they spend and make money. In this learning activity, students make connections between earning and spending money and planning for larger expenses.

Time Frame: 90 minutes

Learning Objectives: Learner will

- define human capital and give examples of it
- explain how human capital is related to career choices, opportunities, and income

- define opportunity cost and give examples of it
- discuss financial behavior
- create a budget plan using a spreadsheet

Information Literacy Standards:

- Access information.
- Evaluate and compare information sources.
- Synthesize information.
- Communicate information by representing it in a spreadsheet.

Digital Literacy Standards:

- Access online information.
- Create a spreadsheet to represent and communicate knowledge.

Common Core State Standards:

- Read closely; cite evidence to support the conclusion.
- Evaluate and integrate content in different formats.
- Gather/assess information from multiple sources.
- Draw evidence from texts to support analysis, reflection, and research.
- Use technology to produce/publish writing and interact/collaborate.
- Use digital media/visual displays of data to express information.

Resources:

- Presentation slides
- Class set of Internet-connected computers with spreadsheet program and demo computer station with projector

Planning for Diverse Learners:

- Have students work in pairs (one typical and one with needs, such as language or physical limitations).
- Have students share equipment if there is limited access to it.
- Provide a choice of information sources.
- Provide more structure for the task or divide the steps into substeps.
- Topics may be sensitive for some students, so they should be able to choose their topics.

Instructional Strategies and Learning Activities:

1. Ask students how they might get money to pay for things (e.g., allowance, gifts of money, asking parents for money, work for money).
2. Ask students what they spend money on (e.g., food, entertainment, transportation, clothes), and create a class list of expenses. Add "savings" to the list for longer-term items.
3. Ask students to share additional recommendations for responsible money management. A student may mention budgeting.
4. In small groups, ask students to discuss money-choice situations. Ask students to report on their conclusions, and lead a class discussion about money-management priorities. (Optional activity)
5. Explain the concept of a budget: planning how to spend money based on a person's needs for both short- and longer-term needs. Lead a class discussion on the benefits of budgeting and saving.
6. Demonstrate how to make a week's budget plan using a spreadsheet program. List anticipated items in the first column (based on the class list), the days of the week in columns B–H (2–8), and a total column. Input sample numbers using copying functions as appropriate, and total the expenses using the add function. Ask students how they can keep records of their spending (e.g., home-computer spreadsheet, mobile app, paper spreadsheet, ledger). Encourage students to consult newspaper ads in order to get accurate costs.
7. Ask each student to create their own budget plan using a spreadsheet. Note that students' available funding may differ significantly, so tell students that they can do a "pretend" budget.
8. Ask students to pair-share their budgets.
9. Discuss with the class their findings and insights. Did any of them create a budget that was larger than the amount of money that they receive? Lead a discussion on how they might get more money; for example, the fact that they have made a budget can be used as a way to "sell" their parents on getting or increasing their allowance. If they cannot increase their budget, brainstorm with them ways to reduce spending.

Variations:

- Do just steps 1–5 or just steps 6–9.
- Ask students to generate money-management problem scenarios for each other to address.
- Based on their week's budget, ask students to create a month-long budget (make each week one column).
- Ask students to create bar charts of their budgets and compare them with their peers.

- Ask students to reduce their budget by 10% and have them manipulate their figures so that they add up to the reduced total. They should explain their choices and the impact that those choices have on their lifestyle.
- Teach students about compound interest, and ask students to investigate how savings can increase with different percentages of interest over time.
- Ask students to locate, critique, and compare free mobile spreadsheet and budget apps.
- Use alternative websites:

  - https://www.practicalmoneyskills.com/foreducators/lesson_plans/lev_2/2_1.pdf
  - http://www.pacareerstandards.com/documents/Bar-Graph-This-Budget-SAS-27774.doc
  - http://www.pathwaytofinancialsuccess.org/wp-content/uploads/2014/04/Discover_MS-Lesson-2_Record-Keeping.pdf
  - http://gazillionaire.com
  - http://www.themint.org/kids/

Student Assessment: Students' budgets are evaluated in terms of the plan's feasibility and spreadsheet skills (see table 7.1).

Table 7.1.　Rubric

	Introductory 0–1	Acceptable 2–3	Proficient 4–5	Score
Layout	Layout is unorganized. Data are not labeled. Cells are not formatted.	Layout organization is somewhat logical, but parts are unclear. A few errors in labeling or cell formatting exist.	Layout is organized in a clear and logical manner. Data are clearly labeled in columns and rows. Cells are formatted correctly. No spelling errors.	
Content	Very small data sample does not allow for analysis. No variation in information types.	Sample includes enough data for basic research. Some use of varied information types.	Large data sample allows for advanced research. A variety of information is present (numbers, dates, percentages, text).	
Analysis	Data is not sorted. Many	Data is sorted but not filtered. A few	Data are sorted and filtered to	

	Introductory 0–1	Acceptable 2–3	Proficient 4–5	Score
	formula and function errors. Analysis results are flawed.	errors occur in the formulas and/or functions used.	select appropriate information. Formulas and functions are used correctly to analyze data. Analysis of data provides facts needed.	
Layout Design	Little or no layout design. No chart or graph is present.	Layout design is generally appropriate for the task. Some variety of font sizes and style. Chart or graph may be incomplete.	Layout design is appropriate to task. Use of borders, varied fonts and font styles, and alignment of data enhance data presentation. Charts or graphs are incorporated to aid visual interpretation of data.	
Chart/ Graph	No chart or graph is present.	Chart or graph has some labeling errors. Chart or graph may be inappropriate for the type of information being presented.	Chart or graph is clearly labeled (title, legend, x and y axis) and easy to interpret. The chart or graph selected is appropriate for the type of data being presented.	
Total Score				

REPRESENTATIVE LEARNING ACTIVITIES

The following activities can easily involve information and digital literacy. Each topic can jumpstart lesson planning.

Grade 6:

- Compare calligraphy around the world; design an original font.
- Compare constellations of different civilizations.
- Compare the ancient and modern Olympics.

- Compare Disney movie versions of ancient civilizations and other sources of information about the civilizations.
- Compare typhoons and hurricanes.
- Compare volcanoes around the world.
- Create an online cultural artifact museum.
- Create a personal or family budget.
- Photograph examples of math in nature.
- Compare math measurement systems and create one.

Grade 7:

- Role play author panels (e.g., fantasy authors over time, Latino authors, poets by country).
- Develop a visual country "slice of life" spectrum: rural to urban, poor to rich, north to south, dawn to night, young to old, and so forth.
- Calculate the cost of raising a child in different cultures.
- Make a scale model of a landmark.
- Re-create a typical day for a refugee.
- Compare teens by country along multiple dimensions (e.g., demographics, leisure activities, education, dating customs).
- Locate and analyze political cartoons from around the world.
- Analyze culture crashes.
- Compare different countries' newspaper accounts of an event or issue.
- Edit photos or videos to make a point or persuade someone (e.g., the same video footage could promote peace or war, depending on how it is manipulated).

Grade 8:

- Create and test bridges in terms of their structure.
- Create card games about the periodic table elements.
- Visualize the history of arithmetic and algebra in different countries.
- Identify proportions and other math functions related to baseball.
- Create a diary about moving west.
- Compare primary documents about the Civil War (e.g., a soldier's diary, newspaper account, slave narrative).
- Experience a U.S. history simulation (http://socialstudiescentral.com/?q= content/online-interactive-simulations).
- Use primary documents from the 19th century to convince someone to move west (http://www.loc.gov/ammem).
- Create a song about a 19th-century U.S. event.

- Remix movie trailers as different genres (e.g., *Mary Poppins* as a thriller: https://www.youtube.com/watch?v=2T5_0AGdFic).

For more ideas of learning activities, consult http://k12digitalcitizenship. wikispaces.com

CONFIGURATIONS

Ideally, information and digital literacies should be woven into the curriculum fabric seamlessly. However, providing explicit instruction about these literacies enables students to gain important conceptual and procedural knowledge that they can apply to subject matter. To that end, a couple of curricular configurations are suggested to ensure a systematic approach to education for information and digital literacies. The goal is to map each year so that all of the information and digital literacy standards are met by the end of the academic year.

1. Each year four information and digital literacies units are taught, one per quarter, one per major subject (i.e., language arts, social studies, science, math). The following curriculum is a representative example.

Grade 6:

- Language arts literary genre study. Make a genre parody of a myth or legend by creating a podcast or animated movie (e.g., http://digitalfilms. com).
- Mathematics in earth forms. Use a camera to capture examples of shapes, angles, and Fibonacci patterns in earth forms. Students can use drawing tools or photo-editing tools to mark the mathematical aspects.
- Math in advertisements. Generate ratios, statistics, and other math operations from advertisements such as food ads.
- Social studies simulation of a day in ancient civilization. Locate or generate images to create a slideshow (e.g., using https://animoto.com) of a typical day.
- Digital citizenship. Cite courses correctly. Discuss intellectual property after viewing http://www.loc.gov/teachers/copyrightmystery/?#/reading/ and http://www.commoncraft.com.

Grade 7:

- Language arts literary world map. Create a world map (e.g., Google Earth) that pinpoints stories from around the world. Each location is marked with an image of the story and a summary that includes setting details.

- Social studies comparison of revolutions. Create a class database to aid in comparing aspects of American, French, Russian, and Latin American revolutions (e.g., time period, length of time, geographic factors, population, communication methods, key people, key events, consequence, links to primary documents).
- Science field guide. Create and play a class card game for plants or animals. Each student chooses one animal or plant order or family, gathers/generates images, collates and describes them, and creates a deck of cards with information for each (image on front and class-determined standardized types of information on the back).
- Math party planning. Develop a party budget using a spreadsheet, and create a visual model for the party layout. Make use of http://www.21things4students.net/21/13-dig-the-data/.
- Digital citizenship. Create a media spot advertisement (e.g., poster, infographic, podcast, video) about cyberbullying. This project can be linked to mathematics (infographic about cyberbullying statistics or students survey peers about cyberbullying incidence), science (physiology of cyberbullying such as hormones, brain responses, etc.), language arts (interviewing skills, "scripting" responses, use of language, communication skills), or social studies (societal issues, disabilities); see https://www.commonsensemedia.org/cyberbullying.

Grade 8:

- Language arts dialect study. Analyze and compare English dialects as they are spoken (http://www.loc.gov/collections/american-english-dialect-recordings-from-the-center-for-applied-linguistics/about-this-collection/ and http://www.dialectsarchive.com/globalmap) and written (http://memory.loc.gov/ammem/amsshtml/amsstitlindex.html).
- Social studies and digital citizenship. What is a citizen? Research the rights and responsibilities of a citizen in U.S. history, comparing them with digital citizen rights and responsibilities. Create a graphic organizer to compare findings.
- Science simulation. Explore and explain physics concepts by using simulations (https://phet.colorado.edu/en/simulations/category/by-level/middle-school).
- Math. Find mathematical functions through coding (http://www.crunchzilla.com/code-monster).

The resultant curriculum map can look like table 7.2:

Table 7.2a. Middle School Curriculum Map: 6th–7th Grades

	6th Grade Topics					7th Grade Topics		
	Ancient day	Math in earth forms	Math ads	Myth parody	Revolution database	Card game	Party plan	Literary world map
IL gain info	locate images	visual data gather	newspaper	research	research	research, locate images	research	research
IL use	analysis	analysis	content analysis	analysis	database to analyze	card formatting	spreadsheet analysis	map stories
IL share	slideshow			podcast, animation	database	card game	spreadsheet, model	map stories
IL personal			shopping			item choice	party	stories
DL create	slideshow	photos		podcast, animation	database	card game	spreadsheet	map
DL communicate	slideshow	photos		podcast, animation	database	show process	spreadsheet, model	map
DL research	locate images	take photos	online newspaper		Internet, database	Internet	Internet	Internet
DL think/solve	locate images	image editing	calculator		database		spreadsheet	map
DL citizen	copyright			copyright	cyberbully, disabilities	cyberbully	cyberbully	copyright
DL tools	Internet, animation	camera, image editing	calculator	podcast, animation	Internet, database	camera, publishing	Internet, spreadsheet	Google Earth

Table 7.2b.   Middle School Curriculum Map: 8th Grade and Capstone

	8th Grade Topics				Capstone
	Citizen rights	Physics simulation	Coding	Compare dialects	Career issue
IL gain info	search strategy	Hypothesis testing	Hypothesis testing	primary sources	research, interview
IL use	analysis	experiment	experiment	content analysis	design process
IL share	graphic organizer				video
IL personal			image choice		career choice
DL create	graphic organizer		coding		video
DL communicate	graphic organizer				video
DL research	Internet	simulation	coding	Internet	research
DL think/solve	graphic organizer	simulation	coding		design process
DL citizen	rights/responsibilities				ethics/legal issue
DL tools	graphic organizer	simulation	coding	Internet (visual, sound)	video

2. Information and digital literacy activities can be done one day per week or one day per month. This model works best for teaching procedural knowledge, such as creating a spreadsheet or editing visual images. Technology tool specialists can cover the basics, and students can explore additional features without having to pay attention to academics. For instance, students can learn how to make a PowerPoint using their own life experiences as the content. To optimize this approach, learning how to use a digital tool should be followed closely by academic assignments that involve the relevant tool to create a content-rich product.

3. A one quarter elective enables students to investigate the information society and experience an entire research process, enhanced by incorporating technology at each stage. An effective context is the world of work. Particularly as middle school can focus on academic procedures, an elective that enables students to do a research project that focuses on career exploration can help them plan for high school and beyond. The following course addresses these skills. Other college/career readiness courses may be found at http://www.fldoe.org/academics/college-career-planning/educators-toolkit/index.stml.

INVESTIGATING CAREERS

This nine-week course enables students to explore an interest that can lead to a career and learn how to conduct research.

Learning Objectives: Learners will

- assess themselves along several dimensions
- relate careers to individual interests, abilities, and aptitudes
- locate and extract information about careers from a variety of resources in different formats
- analyze the relationship between career choices and career preparation opportunities
- identify a challenge that might be encountered in a career, and explain how to solve the issue

Information Literacy Standards:

- Gain knowledge.
- Use and apply knowledge.
- Share knowledge.
- Pursue personal and esthetic growth.

Digital Literacy Standards:

- Use creative thinking and innovative technology.
- Use digital media and environments to communicate and collaborate.
- Apply digital tools fluently to plan, organize, and gather information to evaluate and analyze.
- Use critical thinking to research, manage projects, solve problems, and make informed decisions using technology.
- Practice digital citizenship.
- Use technology proficiently.

Common Core State Standards:

- Conduct research projects.
- Gather/assess information from multiple sources.
- Read closely and cite evidence to support conclusions.
- Assess point of view and purpose to shape text content and style.
- Evaluate/integrate content in different formats.
- Prepare/participate in a range of conversations/collaborations.
- Use technology to produce/publish writing and interact/collaborate.
- Write informative/explanatory texts.
- Produce clear, coherent writing.
- Use correct grammar and usage.
- Use correct spelling, punctuation, and capitalization.

Resources:

- Technology: demo Internet-connected computer with data projector and screen; class set of Internet-connected computers, all of which should have the capability for online journaling/blogging
- Handouts: print out or otherwise make available handouts and other documents noted for each week

Planning for Diverse Learners:

- Have students work in pairs (one typical and one with needs, such as language or physical limitations).
- Have students share equipment if there is limited access to it.
- Provide a choice of information sources.
- Provide more structure for the task or divide the steps into substeps.
- Topics may be sensitive for some students, so they should be able to choose their topics.

Assessments:

- Observe student participation and collaboration in terms of engagement, following directions, and communicating effectively.
- Assess students' decision-making processes and conclusions in terms of appropriateness and productivity.
- Critique student journals/blogs in terms of following directions, the thoroughness and appropriateness of their notes and insights, and in terms of their writing skills.
- Observe students' technological competency in navigating the Internet, locating online resources, managing information, and using social media effectively and responsibly.

Instructional Strategies and Learning Activities:

Week 1: Finding Your Bliss

1. Lead a class discussion about setting goals and achieving them. Ask students to suggest a couple of goals. Explain that goals should be SMART: specific, measurable, attainable, relevant, time-framed. Ask students to give one to two examples of goals that are *not* SMART and goals that are SMART. See http://www.mcas. k12.in.us/Page/4813, which has several resources.
2. Ask students to take the self-assessments at http://www. educationplanner.org/students/self-assessments/index.shtml.
3. Ask students to start a journal or blog (see http://kidslearntoblog. com/45-best-blogging-sites-for-kids/ for possible platforms). Ask them to write about how the results of their self-assessments can drive their goal setting.

Week 2: Identifying Career Clusters

1. Ask students to write a scenario or draw a picture of themselves and their life 5 years from now and 10 years from now.
2. Have students access and sign into http://www.cacareerzone.org. Have them do the Explore section "Assess yourself." Alternatively, use http://www.educationplanner.org/students/career-planning/ find-careers/career-clusters-activity.shtml.
3. Ask students to choose two careers within a job family to explore for the rest of the unit.
4. Group students by job family, and ask them to compare their findings. Ask students to journal their insights.

Week 3: Exploring Careers

1. Ask the class to generate questions that they might have about a career (e.g., salary, training needed, demand).
2. Ask students to access and sign into http://www.cacareerzone.org. Ask them to do the Explore section "Occupations," comparing two careers. Have students click on "View occupations."
3. Ask students to make a table to record aspects of each job for their journal/blog:

ASPECT	JOB 1	JOB 2
Description		
Aspect 2 . . .		

4. Ask students to compare findings with another resource, such as http://www.onetonline.org/find/, http://www.labormarketinfo.edd. ca.gov/, http://www.bls.gov/k12/, adding information to their table.

Week 4: Making a Career Real

1. Lead a class discussion about information that can be gleaned from video interviews about individuals in different careers (e.g., demographic information, appearance, career planning, career ladder, preparation, typical activities, advice). Develop a class list of details to look for.
2. Ask students to locate videos of career interviews. Good websites to explore include

    http://www.careeronestop.org/videos/careerandclustervideos/
      career-and-cluster-videos.aspx
    https://www.iseek.org/careers/careervideos.html
    http://knowitall.scetv.org/careeraisle/students/hs/index.cfm
    http://www.drkit.org/careervideos/
    http://www.pbs.org/newshour/extra/2014/04/the-stories-
      behind-22-stem-superstars/
    http://thefutureschannel.com

3. Ask students to journal their insights and share their insights with a peer in the same career cluster.
4. Ask the class: "What other information do you want to know? How might you find the answers?"

Week 5: Choosing a Field of Study

1. Lead a class discussion about preparing for a career. Ask the class to generate a list of different kinds of education and training one might need in order to be prepared to enter a career (e.g., appren-

tice, internship, on-the-job training, junior college, bachelor's degree, advanced degree, technical training).

2. Have students access https://www1.cfnc.org/Plan/For_High_ School/_default.aspx. Ask students to start an account. Mention that their families can also have a free account.

3. Ask students to go to the High School Planning tab. Ask them to complete the "Planning my career goals while in high school" block of information.

4. Ask them to complete the "Your plan of study" block of information based on career clusters that align with their interests and abilities.

5. Ask students to choose a pathway related to that cluster and click on a program of study.

6. Ask students to examine and save the course of study to their online account site. Also ask them to copy the course of study into their journal/blog.

7. Debrief the class in terms of findings and insights. Ask students to journal about how this information impacts their plans for high school and their career.

Week 6: Gaining Knowledge Outside of Class

1. Lead a class discussion about cocurricular activities after defining that term. Ask students how they think cocurricular activities can help them prepare for their careers. For instance, students might join the drama club if they want to go into the entertainment industry, or they might want to be a lab aide if they want to go into chemical engineering. Ask student volunteers to share some of their experiences in cocurricular activities. Ask the class to brainstorm other possible cocurricular activities that might interest them and help them prepare for their careers.

2. Ask half of the students to access the web portal of their intended high school and locate information about the school's cocurricular activities. Ask the other half of the students to access community websites (e.g., Chamber of Commerce, library, local government, parks and recreation) to locate cocurricular opportunities. Remind students to cite their sources.

3. Assign students into groups of four: two who researched high school websites and two who researched community websites. Ask them to compare their lists. Then have them create a comprehensive list of cocurricular activities and generate a list of possible questions about the activities.

4. If possible, invite high school students to discuss representative cocurricular opportunities in the school and community. Have them state how their participation helps them develop workplace skills and prepare for their careers. Ask each group to pose questions about cocurricular activities.

5. Ask each student to journal/blog about two school and two community opportunities that they might want to join and state how these choices will help them prepare for their careers.

Week 7: Making a Career Public Service Announcement (PSA)

1. Lead a class discussion about the use of commercials (e.g., inform, persuade, motivate). Ask the class what makes an effective commercial (e.g., attention grabbing, connects with the audience, good visuals, clear succinct message, emotional appeal, memorable, convincing, call to action). PSAs are messages in the public interest. PSAs about careers can help the viewer to learn more about possible careers of interest.

2. Share this video about making PSAs: https://www.youtube.com/watch?v=eywBa0xfQFw.

3. Demonstrate how to make a short PSA using iMovie or Windows Movie Maker. Share video creation tips at https://vimeo.com/videoschool/101.

4. Ask students in pairs to create a 30-second PSA on one career or career cluster using the information that they have gathered throughout the learning module.

5. Ask students to share their PSAs and critique a peer's PSA using this rubric: http://www.rock-your-world.org/website/PSAs/PSA%20Task%20Sheet%20and%20Project%20Rubric.pdf.

6. Ask students to journal about their experiences.

Week 8: Challenges of the Job

1. Lead a class discussion about challenges on the job. "What might be some challenges or dilemmas that one might encounter in many workplaces?" (e.g., interpersonal conflicts, lack of resources, too much or too little work to do, low wages). "What might be some legal or ethical dilemmas in different careers?" (e.g., fraud, cheating, slander, bribes, prejudice, issues of confidentiality or privacy, value conflicts such as euthanasia, risky scientific advances). Ethics might need to be explained: doing the right thing. Share the video https://www.youtube.com/watch?v=vstg5c3c3g8. If you

have time, watch and discuss this video on business ethics scenarios: https://www.youtube.com/watch?v=sDPsSyaZNIw.

2. State that some careers have codes of ethics, which provide guidance on right behavior. Share and discuss Page 8 of this ethics project lesson: http://www5.milwaukee.k12.wi.us/school/hamilton/files/2014/05/Ethics-Everyone-Else-Does-It.pdf.

3. Ask students to research an ethical or legal dilemma for one of their career choices and find out how to resolve the dilemma. Some of the videos for Week 4 might address some issues. Encourage them to find a code of ethics for their career field.

4. Ask student pairs to role play their ethical or legal career dilemma. Have peers assess the role play using the rubric found at https://iportfolio.curtin.edu.au/examples/role_playing.cfm.

5. Ask the class to compare ethical dilemmas and their resolutions across career clusters. Ask students to journal about ethical aspects of their chosen career.

Week 9: Interviewing Skills

1. Lead a class discussion about the importance of interviewing as a way to gain information and understanding. "When you interview for a job or volunteer work, both you and your potential boss are gaining information about each other, the job itself, and the working environment."

2. Share the video https://www.youtube.com/watch?v=dWodxAdsGvY. Divide the class into their career clusters. Ask half of the students in each cluster to focus on the applicant and the other half to focus on the employer. After viewing the video, debrief with the class regarding their insights about interviewing.

3. Ask the applicant half of the class to generate questions for the employers, and ask the employer half to generate questions for the applicants.

4. Distribute and discuss the interviewing skills handout (http://www.cccoe.net/social/PVSinterviewing.htm) to the class.

5. Divide the class into career clusters. Within those clusters, create groups of four: two applicants and two employees each. Making use of the information researched throughout the career module and the generated interview questions. Ask one student (employer) to interview a student applicant, and ask the other pair to critique the interview using the handout guidelines. Then switch pairs. Share feedback within the group of four.

6. Debrief the class about their interview experiences and insights. Ask them to journal about their thoughts about interviewing and their career choices.
7. Lead a class review about the career module. "How have your goals and their strategies to achieving them changed? How have your knowledge and attitude about careers changed? What information and digital literacy skills have you gained? What are your next steps?"

IMPLICATIONS FOR SCHOOL LIBRARIANS

As noted in earlier chapters, school librarians should participate early in curriculum development and throughout instructional design and implementation. Fortunately, current attention to college/career readiness, Common Core State Standards, and Next Generation Science Standards can be leveraged in order to highlight the importance of information and digital literacies. At each stage of curriculum planning and use, school librarians can share their expertise. Even when teachers bring in their students for a learning activity that has not been reviewed by the school librarian ahead of time, it is usually easy to find a way to "translate" part of the lesson into information literacy terminology in order to raise the awareness of classroom teachers and students. School librarians should also debrief learning activities with classroom teachers in order to find ways to deepen knowledge and skill of information and digital literacy in future learning opportunities.

Chapter Eight

Model Curriculum for High School

This chapter provides a scope-and-sequence curriculum for Grades 9–12. It offers two model stand-alone courses (one for ninth graders and one for senior students) with sample modules/units and learning activities. It also suggests different configurations for delivering curriculum and notes how modules can be incorporated into the existing academic curriculum.

CONTENT

In high school, students explore discipline-specific ways to gain and create knowledge. They also make connections between disciplines and to real-world situations. With their emphasis on selecting and using a variety of processes and intellectual tools to match tasks, information and digital literacies facilitate both in-depth and broad-based learning. Working across all curricula and networking with the community, school librarians are centrally positioned to collaborate with the entire school community in order to provide the conditions for optimum learning: relevant and developmentally appropriate curriculum and supporting resources, welcoming and stimulating learning environments, and effective instruction.

Information literacy encompasses several performance indicators for high schoolers:

- *Planning:* Follow an inquiry-based process for seeking knowledge; make real-world connections.
- *Accessing information:* Access and use a range of resources effectively; read widely and fluently; explore real-world genres; manage personal knowledge effectively.

- *Evaluation:* Evaluate resources in various formats, noting agenda, values, and context along with accuracy, validity, and appropriateness; challenge ideas.
- *Manipulation:* Use a variety of technology and other information tools to analyze and manage information effectively; apply knowledge to academics and real-world situations; build a conceptual framework; create knowledge.
- *Communication:* Publish and copyright original knowledge in various formats to various audiences appropriately; present professionally; participate collaboratively as a member of a learning network.
- *Using a domain-specific approach to research* (e.g., think like a social scientist).

Likewise, digital literacy encompasses several performance indicators for high schoolers:

- *Technology operations:* Install and troubleshoot various technologies.
- *Use of technology and information tools:* Select and use a variety of technology and information tools for academic and real-world tasks.
- *Digital citizenship:* Model and teach digital citizenship; contribute to physical and digital communities (e.g., service learning, citizen journalist, scientist citizen).

These general indicators are particularized in various subject matter and types of learning activities and applications, also taking into account the growing diversification of learners as they develop and mature. Particularly since high schoolers have more individualized course plans and can usually take electives, having grade-level benchmarks becomes unruly. Ultimately, students need to have a broad repertoire of intellectual tools that they can select and use in order to address the various situations that they encounter in academia and daily life.

SAMPLE LEARNING ACTIVITIES

In high school, information literacy can be explored as an intellectual construct as well as a set of practices in interacting with information. This sample learning activity exemplifies this approach.

Learning Activity: Information Cycle Flowchart

Overview: Over 100,000 books are published yearly, and that's just in the United States. It is amazing how much digital information is generated every minute. Ideas are "free" and ubiquitous. How are those ideas expressed and recorded? One way to look at information is in terms of its cycle: from its creation to its dissemination, access, and use. Information can also be considered in terms of its "life" from the time that an event occurs to its recording and impact. Technology intersects at several points. In this learning activity, students trace a piece of information from its inception to its end.

Time Frame: Two to three class periods

Learning Objectives: Learner will

- trace the information cycle of a piece of information
- create a flowchart that shows the information cycle

Information Literacy Standards:

- Access information.
- Evaluate and compare information sources.
- Synthesize information.
- Communicate information by representing it in a flowchart.

Digital Literacy Standards:

- Access online information.
- Create a flowchart using a graphic organizer in order to represent and communicate knowledge.

Common Core State Standards:

- Conduct research projects.
- Gather/assess information from multiple sources.
- Analyze text structures.
- Read closely; cite evidence to support conclusions.
- Assess point of view and purpose in order to shape text content and style.
- Compare texts' content and approach.
- Evaluate/integrate content in different formats.
- Draw evidence from texts to support analysis, reflection, and research.
- Use digital media/visual displays of data to express information/enhance understanding.
- Write informative/explanatory texts.
- Produce clear, coherent writing.
- Use correct grammar and usage.
- Use correct spelling, punctuation, and capitalization.
- Understand language functions in different contexts.
- Use a range of academic and domain-specific words and phrases.

Resources:

- Technology: demo Internet-connected computer with data projector and screen; class set of Internet-connected computers, all of which should have flowchart tools (e.g., Inspiration,http://www.eduplace.com/graphicorganizer/orhttp://office.microsoft.com/en-us/word-help/draw-flowcharts-with-word-and-powerpoint-HA001055266.aspx).

Planning for Diverse Learners:

- Have students work in pairs (one typical and one with needs, such as language or physical limitations).
- Have students share equipment if there is limited access to it.
- Provide a choice of information sources.
- Provide more structure for the task or divide the steps into substeps.
- Topics may be sensitive for some students, so they should be able to choose their topics.

Instructional Strategies and Learning Activities:

1. Prepare for the lesson by locating and downloading the infographic on data: http://aci.info/2014/07/12/the-data-explosion-in-2014-minute-by-minute-infographic/. Review all of the links mentioned in the lesson to know the content and to make sure that the links work.
2. Ask students to recall the September 11, 2001, event. What do they remember? Ask them to think about some of these questions, and have a few students share their thoughts.

   - Who witnessed that event, and how did they record their experiences?
   - With whom did they share that information—and why?
   - When news outlets gather information about an event, which sources do they trust—and why? What information do they select and discard—and why? The agenda of each news outlet or any other communications channel impacts what information is shared, as well as when and how.
   - How did people react to the information, and how did they act on it? September 11 resulted in tighter security, probably the reelection of George W. Bush, and the PATRIOT Act.
   - How has information about September 11 changed over the months and years?

3. Show students the website and video about information cycles: http://www.library.illinois.edu/ugl/howdoi/informationcycle.html or https://www2.humboldt.edu/libraryquiz/knowledge-cycle.
4. Explain that one way to represent an information cycle is with a flow chart. Show them http://www.rff.com/how_to_draw_a_flowchart.htm or https://www.moresteam.com/toolbox/process-flow-chart.cfm.
5. Ask students to choose an event and research its information cycle. Ask them to make a flowchart of the resultant information cycle.

Variations:

• Create a flow chart of an information product (e.g., radio show, magazine issue, podcast, piece of sheet music, band recording).
• Create an information cycle flowchart that traces a piece of information from the creator to the target audience, noting how the information is produced, disseminated, accessed, and used by the audience.

Student Assessments appear in table 8.1.

Table 8.1. Student Assessment

Criteria	Introductory 0–1 points	Acceptable 2–3 points	Proficient 4 points	Score
Accuracy	The flowchart content does not reflect the realities of the information cycle.	The flowchart generally represents the main elements of the information cycle.	The flowchart accurately represents all of the critical elements of the information cycle and their relationships.	x 2
Thoroughness	The flowchart does not convey the logical relationships among the conceptual components.	The flowchart in general shows the logical relationships among most components but has some omissions.	The flowchart captures all of the relationships among all of the conceptual components.	x 1.5
Alignment with Information Cycle	The flowchart does not align with the information cycle.	The flowchart generally aligns with the information cycle.	The flowchart clearly aligns with the information cycle.	x 1.5
Use of Flowchart Schema	Positioning of symbols is not used to convey	The flowchart in general shows the logical	The flowchart captures all of the logical	x 2

Criteria	Introductory 0–1 points	Acceptable 2–3 points	Proficient 4 points	Score
	overall relationships or meaning and links are missing and unlabeled. The flowchart is difficult to understand.	relationships among most components but has some omissions. The appearance of the flowchart is somewhat cluttered or unclear.	relationships among all of the conceptual components. The author has taken full advantage of the medium to engage the reader and to convey ideas.	
Total Score				

Representative Learning Activities

The following activity topics can easily involve information and digital literacy. Each topic can jumpstart lesson planning.

Grade 9:

- Create a word family tree.
- Create a movie trailer or podcast commercial for a book.
- Create an e-book parody of a children's story.
- Compare different types of maps (and print versus digital) to determine how different kinds of information are represented.
- Map how disease is spread.
- Create and play a visual dictionary game with science terms.
- Do postage stamp algebra.
- Act out computer operations.
- Determine what computers can do better than human and worse than humans.
- Maintain a daily blog about your personal information and technology world.

Grade 10:

- Study censorship cases around the world.
- Analyze speeches about freedom.
- Rewrite a play as a news cast.
- Trace the migration of food, both in terms of history and in marketing.
- Create a card game about biomes.
- Calculate sports action on different planets.
- Analyze the math of cartography.

- Analyze the digital divide and make recommendations about how to bridge the divide.
- Create a digital code of ethics.
- Create a Turing test.

Grade 11:

- Create a database about local government agencies.
- Create a time line about voting patterns or legislation.
- Create a digital exhibit about popular culture by decade.
- Create an audio history of U.S. literature.
- Track the decomposition of trash.
- Visualize a day in the life of a chemist.
- Shadow a crime scene investigation.
- Create a game based on chemistry experiments.
- Track satellite orbits using trigonometry.
- Analyze your digital footprint and take steps to improve it.

Grade 12:

- Create a graphic novel (using iComic or ComicLife) about a piece of literature.
- Analyze social media regarding a contemporary event in terms of the representativeness and authority of the author(s). Determine whether the individual was an actual witness. Determine the author's bias.
- Analyze information and digital access and skills needed for e-government resources and services.
- Analyze political campaigns (http://www.livingroomcandidate.org/lessons).
- Give tips about savvy shopping online (see http://www.21things4students.net/21/buyer-beware/).
- Analyze the physics of science fiction stories.
- Analyze the body as a machine in terms of physics.
- Modify a video game to show—or modify—physics principles.
- Create and analyze surveys.
- Participate as a citizen scientist.

For more learning activities ideas, consult http://k12digitalcitizenship.wikispaces.com.

CONFIGURATIONS

1. Each year four information and digital literacies units are taught, one per quarter, one per major subject (i.e., language arts, social studies, science, math). The following curriculum is a representative example. It should be noted that only the core academic subjects are included because graduation expectations have to be based on required courses. Students should be encouraged to explore additional subjects and exceed the lowest common denominator of graduation requirements. Learning is an open-ended realm of experiences.

Grade 9:

- Language arts poem transformation. Choose a poem that resonates with the learner and transform it into another format (e.g., short story, play, series of images).
- Social studies story map. Take a real or virtual trip and narrate what happens along the way. Use a GPS system to identify the exact location of each landmark along the trip. Note how geography impacts the area by using an interactive map (e.g., Google Earth) to pinpoint and annotate landmarks. (See http://edcommunity.esri.com/Resources/ArcLessons/Lessons/T/the-15-minute-storymap, GPS tutorial: http://www.trimble.com/gps_tutorial/.)
- Science wellness plan. Research nutrition and exercise plans. Use a spreadsheet to create a weekly wellness plan. Create additional wellness plans for other populations (e.g., age, culture). (See http://www.healthyeating.org/Healthy-Kids/Kids-Games-Activities/TeenBEAT.aspx.)
- Math energy audit and digital citizenship. Research energy costs and ways to cut down on energy use. Audit home energy use, including utility bills. Note tiered costs for energy use (i.e., when more water is used the per unit cost is higher). Develop algebraic functions to calculate costs (especially tiers) and means to cut down on energy costs. Energy costs and use can inputted into a spreadsheet and graphed.

Grade 10:

- Language arts content analysis of newspapers. Compare newspapers from different countries in terms of layout, fonts, headlines, sections and features, prioritized articles, length of articles, and use of language. Create a comparative table.
- Social studies technology-enhanced international summit simulation. Simulate an international summit, such as the United Nations or global warming summit. The class chooses an international issue to resolve (UNESCO

lists several), with each group representing a different country. Groups research the issue from their country's point of view (i.e., business, farming, government, etc.), noting technology impact, and create a PowerPoint or equivalent to present their perspective at the summit simulation. Groups discuss and hopefully resolve the issue, ideally incorporating technology. This learning activity could be done among classes or among schools in a webinar format.

- Biology field guide database. Choose a local plant or animal to research, using visual searching tools. If possible, take photos of the item. The class develops a list of facts to research about each item and a standardized layout for the information. A class searchable database collates the research.
- Math in architecture. Take photos or locate pictures of architecture; blueprints can also be used. Identify geometric shapes, and generate geometric functions to describe the architectural features. Use a vector drawing tool to transcribe the image and geometric function.

Grade 11:

- Literary digital exhibit. Choose a U.S. novel or nonfiction account. Locate artifacts that provide context for the text (e.g., popular culture, events, people). Curate the artifacts, and create a digital exhibit of them (use Pachyderm or another digital exhibit tool).
- War primary documents. Small groups locate primary documents during a war (e.g., Civil War, Spanish American War, World War I or II, etc.) that reflect different experiences and perspectives; each group could reflect one dimension (e.g., state, type of job, age). Create an annotated e-book of the primary documents. Start with http://www.loc.gov/ammem and http://www.archives.gov for online collections.
- Chemistry product graphic novel. Research a chemical product and how it is produced or manufactured (e.g., nylon, dye, cleaners). Create a graphic novel to show how it is produced.
- Digital seismic wave mathematical analysis. Use digital simulations to analyze seismic waves, such as those created by earthquakes and volcanoes. Generate trigonometric functions and graphs with a graphing calculator to describe and model seismic waves and how they work.

Grade 12:

- Language arts advertising that sells culture. Locate and analyze advertisements of transnational companies (e.g., Nike, Coca-Cola, Nestle, Honda, Disney) in terms of how they incorporate or impact cultures (see http://www.culturalsurvival.org/publications/cultural-survival-quarterly/c-tedivoire/advertising-and-global-culture). Locate articles about this issue, noting media literacy aspects. Create a multimedia presentation that illustrates your point of view about this issue and provides recommendations on how cultures can be maintained.

- Sports physics game. Research the physics aspects of sports (e.g., golf swings, tossing and catching balls, swimming strokes). Calculate and graph physics functions that describe sports aspects. Incorporate the findings into designing or modifying an electronic or video game (e.g., machinima).
- Lying statistics infographic. Research how statistics can be misleading through its mathematical manipulation or its visualization. Research a controversial topic that can have misleading information based on statistical abuse. Create an infographic piece of propaganda using statistical abuse.
- Consumerism. Do comparison shopping. Research the impact of globalization. Compare public and private businesses. Investigate health issues.
- How do advertisers sell culture? Research transnational company marketing strategies that impact local cultures. Locate examples of advertisements that appear to impact local cultures. Create a multimedia presentation (e.g., PowerPoint, animation, movie) that presents the problem, the underlying issues and impacts, and recommendations for ways to maintain the local culture.

The resultant curriculum map can look like table 8.2.

Table 8.2a. High School Curriculum Map: 9th–10th Grades

	9th Grade Topics					10th Grade Topics		
	Story map	Wellness plan	Energy audit	Transform poem into another form	International summit simulation	Biology field guide	Geometry of architecture	Compare newspapers around the world
IL gain	GPS, maps	nutrition, exercise info	energy info	genre features	issue research	biology facts	architecture features	newspaper elements
IL use	calculate location	spreadsheet calculations	functions	transliteracy	construct evidence	analyze biology	analyze math	content analysis
IL share	story map	spreadsheet	audit	transformed poem	speeches	database, camera, Internet	draw math with architecture	table
II personal	neighborhood	wellness plan	save energy	poem choice	personal issue	favorite biology	favorite buildings	section interest
DL create	story map	wellness spreadsheet plan	functions	transformed poem	PPT	database	image overlay	table
DL communicate	story map	spreadsheet plan	audit	transformed poem	PPT	database	visual	table
DL research	local geography and economics	nutrition, exercise info	energy info	genre features	digital resources	Internet, camera	locate architecture	newspapers, media
DL think/solve	story map	calculate plan	analyze energy	transliteracy	graphic organizers	database	drawing tool	"find" feature
DL citizen	contribute to community	self-image	conservation	transliteracy	technology for social good	contribute to community	citing	global perspective
DL tools	GPS software, camera	spreadsheet, Internet	math functions, Internet	digital visual tool, Internet	PPT, Internet, graphic organizers	database, camera, Internet	vector drawing tool, Internet	table, Internet, DB

Table 8.2b. High School Curriculum Map: 11th–12th Grades

	11th Grade Topics					12th Grade Topics		
	War primary documents	*Graphic novel of chem product*	*Seismic waves analysis*	*Literary digital exhibit*	*Supreme Court debate*	*Physics of sports*	*How to lie with statistics*	*How do advertisers sell culture?*
IL gain	online primary documents about war	chem manufacturing, graphic novel features	seismic waves & earth	artifacts of book/era	Supreme Court issues	forces, mechanics, anatomy, sports action, games	statistics, media	culture, media, advertising
IL use	point of view	analyze & transform info	analyze wave simulations mathematically	curate	analyze data	visual analysis	spreadsheet, graphs	content analysis
IL share	e-book	translate into graphic novel	math model	digital exhibit	debate	game	spreadsheet, graphs	multimedia presentation
Il personal	personal point of view	visuals	local shakes	personal interests	topic interest	favorite sport	topic interest	topic interest
DL create	e-book	graphic novel	math model	PPT, e-book	video debate	game	infographic	multimedia presentation
DL communicate	e-book	graphic novel	graphing calculator	digital exhibit	video debate	game	infographic	multimedia presentation
DL research	primary documents	chem manufacturing, graphic novel features	simulations	history, literature, media	Supreme Court issues	physics, sports	statistics, media	media literacy
DL think/ solve	navigate Internet, documents	transliteracy	analyze simulations, use graphing calculator	curate	graphic organizers	visual tool for analysis, game features	spreadsheet, graphs	content analysis
DL citizen	point of view	transliteracy	modeling	citing	social good	contribute to community	media literacy	media literacy
DL tools	e-book, Internet	graphic novel, camera, draw tool	graphing calculator, simulation	digital exhibit tool (e.g., Pachyderm)	video, Internet, DB, graphic organizers	game, Internet	infographic, spreadsheet, graphs, Internet	multimedia presentation tool, Internet

Table 8.2c.   High School Curriculum: Capstone

	Capstone
	Community action research
IL gain	community, local issue, action research
IL use	action research
IL share	action research plan
Il personal	local issue
DL create	action research plan
DL communicate	action research plan
DL research	local issue
DL think/solve	analyze issue
DL citizen	contribute to community
DL tools	varied

2. Information and digital literacy activities can be done one day per week or one day per month. This model works best for teaching procedural knowledge, such as creating a spreadsheet or editing visual images. Technology tool specialists can cover the basics, and students can explore additional features without having to pay attention to academics. For instance, students can learn how to make a graphic novel using their own life experiences as the content. To optimize this approach, learning how to use a digital tool should be followed closely by academic assignments that involve using the relevant tool to create a content-rich product.

3. A one-quarter or one-semester elective enables students to investigate the information society and experience an entire research process, enhanced by incorporating technology at each stage. Two courses are outlined here: The first course is for freshmen or sophomores in order to provide them with a solid grounding on research processes and technology tools. The other course serves as a capstone experience for seniors or advanced juniors. It uses action research as a self-reflective methodology for applying a systematic approach to improve one's community.

I-SEARCH RESEARCH COURSE

The following I-Search research course targets freshmen and sophomore high schoolers and provides instruction in self-reflective research processes that involve a variety of information resources and tools. Educational technology is incorporated throughout the course in order for students to learn and apply the technology. The course is designed as a full-semester offering, similar to a language arts course. If scaled down, it could be embedded into an existing course, such as social studies. The librarian and classroom teacher can determine which content and activities are needed, depending on the student's prior knowledge and the context of the existing course.

Learning Objectives: Learners will

- explain the essential aspects of the reference process, the research interview, and the ethical and legal considerations of information use
- demonstrate how to locate information using traditional and technological approaches
- analyze and apply criteria for selecting reference materials
- analyze the organization of reference service
- develop an I-Search research project
- communicate information effectively

Information Literacy Standards:

- Gain knowledge.
- Use and apply knowledge.
- Share knowledge.
- Pursue personal and esthetic growth.

Digital Literacy Standards:

- Use creative thinking and innovative technology.
- Use digital media and environments to communicate and collaborate.
- Apply digital tools fluently to plan, organize, and gather information to evaluate and analyze information.
- Use critical thinking to research, manage projects, solve problems, and make informed decisions using technology.
- Practice digital citizenship.
- Use technology proficiently.

Common Core State Standards:

- Conduct research projects.
- Gather/assess information from multiple sources.
- Identify main ideas/themes and their development.
- Assess point of view and purpose in order to shape text content and style.
- Compare texts' content and approach.
- Read closely; cite evidence to support conclusions.
- Evaluate/integrate content in different formats.
- Draw evidence from texts to support analysis, reflection, and research.
- Use technology to produce/publish writing and interact/collaborate.
- Write informative/explanatory texts.
- Produce clear, coherent writing.
- Use correct grammar and usage.
- Understand language functions in different contexts.
- Use correct spelling, punctuation, and capitalization.
- Use a range of academic and domain-specific words and phrases.
- Present information that listeners can follow.
- Adapt speech to various contexts and tasks.

Resources:

- Technology: Demo Internet-connected computer with data projector and screen; class set of Internet-connected computers, all of which should have the capability for online journaling/blogging.
- Handouts: Print out or otherwise make available handouts and other documents noted for each week.

Planning for Diverse Learners:

- Have students work in pairs (one typical and one with needs, such as language or physical limitations).
- Have students share equipment if there is limited access to it.
- Provide a choice of information sources.
- Provide more structure for the task or divide the steps into substeps.
- Topics may be sensitive for some students, so they should be able to choose their topics.

Assessments:

- Observe student participation and collaboration in terms of engagement, following directions, and communicating effectively.
- Assess students' oral presentation according to the class checklist.
- Assess students' I-Search report according to the project rubric (http://www.lssc.edu/faculty/julia_l_sweitzer/Shared Documents/I-Search Paper rubric.doc).
- Critique student journals/blogs in terms of following directions, the thoroughness and appropriateness of their notes and insights, and in terms of their writing skills. If students are paired in order to comment on each other's journals, assess their comments for appropriateness and insights.
- Observe students' technological competency in navigating the Internet, locating online resources, managing information, and using social media effectively and responsibly.

Instructional Strategies and Learning Activities:

Week 1: Information Literacy and You
Much of this project will refer to http://libguides.mchenry.edu/tutorial.

1. Tell students that they will be creating an I-Search research project. They will choose a topic of interest to them and research it. In the process, they will journal about their experiences. Share the I-Search project rubric: http://www.lssc.edu/faculty/julia_l_sweitzer/Shared Documents/I-Search Paper rubric.doc.
2. Lead a class discussion about the benefits of journaling. Ask students to start a journal blog (see http://kidslearntoblog.com/45-best-blogging-sites-for-kids/ for possible platforms). Consider pairing students so that they can comment on each other's journal throughout the project.
3. Ask students to do a quick-write journal entry on information literacy and research. State: "Drawing on your own knowledge, (1)

define *information literacy*, (2) describe how you do research, and (3) describe how you feel when you do research."

4. Share and explain the American Association of School Librarians (AASL) learning standards (http://www.ala.org/aasl/standards-guidelines/learning-standards). Ask student volunteers to provide an example of each standard that they may have done.
5. Show students the first web page of the McHenry County College information literacy tutorial: http://libguides.mchenry.edu/content. php?pid=528044&sid=4344264. Define the term *information literacy* , and explain how research is part of information literacy but is not equal to it (e.g., reading a book or viewing a movie is part of information literacy but does not have to be research).
6. Share one or more research process models (http://ictnz.com/infolitmodels.htm , https://vickipalmer.wordpress.com/knowledge/information-seeking/). Depending on the knowledge base of students, small groups of students could choose one research model for their course.
7. Explain to students that research has its emotional aspects. Share Kuhlthau's Information Searching Process image (https://vickipalmer.wordpress.com/knowledge/information-seeking/). Another reason to journal is to capture those feelings and think about them.
8. Ask students to choose two topics by the beginning of Week 2.

Week 2: Developing a Research Strategy

1. Review the I-Search project. Ask students to take one of their two topics of interest and list what they know and what they want to know in their journal. This will begin their research plan. Refer to http://libguides.mchenry.edu/content.php?pid=528044&sid=4345373.
2. Lead a class discussion on generating research questions. Refer to http://libguides.mchenry.edu/content.php?pid=528044&sid=4345497.
3. Disseminate an index card to each student and ask them to write their names in the card's corner. Ask students to create a research question from each of their chosen topics. Ask students to exchange cards and critique them as to the quality of the question; they should then revise their question accordingly.
4. Lead a class discussion about keywords. Refer to Step 4 in http://libguides.mchenry.edu/content.php?pid=528044&sid=4345497, and show the video about selecting keywords. Ask students to circle the keywords on their cards.

5. Remind the class that different sources may use different keywords, usually synonyms. Therefore, ask students to use a thesau-
   rus (even if it's just the feature in word processors) to list synonyms of their keywords in their journal.

Week 3: Information Management

1. The blog journal is a chronological method of keeping track of the
   information that students find (or do not find) and their experiences
   and thoughts in the process. Lead a class discussion about managing their research process, especially in taking notes (extracting
   information) and organizing them (e.g., printing out information
   and highlighting important parts, using index cards, taking photos,
   taking Cornell notes, using a loose-leaf binder).
2. Review note-taking procedures, such as paraphrasing, using keywords, and so forth. Refer to http://library.sasaustin.org/
   noteTaking.php as needed.
3. Show the class a short document and show how to take notes on it.
   Give students another example to practice note taking, and have
   them either compare notes as a pair or provide them with an exem-
   plar to explain how note taking is done.
4. Lead a class discussion about intellectual property, starting with
   the idea of copying someone else's work and calling it your own.
   Define intellectual property as the ownership of recorded ideas and
   the rights associated with that ownership, such as distribution and
   reimbursement for using them. State: "When building on other
   people's work (i.e., recorded ideas), remember to give them credit
   and cite them accurately. Citing resources that you use also helps
   you—and others—to locate and use those resources in the future."
   Show the video https://www.commoncraft.com/video/plagiarism
   as needed. Share examples of plagiarism and acceptable citations:
   https://www.indiana.edu/~istd/examples.html.
5. Review correct citation styles. Show the parts of a citation (http://
   www2.liu.edu/cwis/cwp/library/workbook/evaluate.htm#citing).
   Explain that using a standardized method facilitates locating the
   source. Ask students to identify the parts of a couple of sample
   citations.
6. Show students how to use an online citation tool such as Citation
   Machine   (http://elearningindustry.com/14-best-online-
   bibliography-and-citation-tools). Guides for citing resources are
   also   available   (e.g.,   http://www2.liu.edu/cwis/cwp/library/
   workshop/citation.htm). Ask students to "transform" the sample

citations into an online citation tool and see how the citation is generated.
7. Ask students to journal about how they plan to manage their information management for the I-Search project.

Week 4: Locating Books and Other Documents

1. Ask the class to brainstorm possible sources of information to answer their research question. Referring to http://libguides.mchenry. edu/content.php?pid=528044&sid=4345500, lead a class discussion about the usefulness of different sources of information for different kinds of research questions. Ask students to list in their journal at least a few types of resources to answer each of their research questions.
2. Lead a class discussion about searching for information. Refer to http://libguides.mchenry.edu/content.php?pid=528044&sid= 4345503.
3. Explain that library catalogs are databases that describe and list information "containers" such as books, journals, and other documents. Each item/entry/record in a database includes consistent data about the information: each element is called a "field." Users can locate resources by title, author, subject, and keywords. Those consistent fields enable the user to sort and find/retrieve information. Most school and public libraries use the Dewey Decimal Classification (DDC) system to arrange resources by topic. Review that the location "address" is the call number, which appears on the document's spine. For more details about DDC, refer to http:// www.oclc.org/dewey/versions/ddc22print/intro.pdf.
4. Ask students to find at least one item that can be located using the library catalog. In some school libraries, nonprint resources such as DVDs and e-books are catalogued. Remind students that sometimes a resource may have just one chapter or scene about the desired research topic; for instance, there might not be a whole book on sunflowers, but a book on flowers is likely to have some information. Therefore, a broader term might have to be used.
5. Lead a class discussion about evaluating resources: "With so much information available in so many ways, it's important to be able to choose which information to believe and use." Ask students how they determine the quality of the resources that they locate. Refer to http://libguides.mchenry.edu/content.php?pid=528044&sid= 4345526. State: "One of the advantages of library collections is that they are selected by librarians, so the resources are reviewed and support the curriculum."

6. Ask students to explain the basis for their choice of books, aligned with evaluation criteria. Ask them to journal about their decision-making process.

Week 5: Locating Articles

1. Ask students how they typically find documents such as articles within a magazine.
2. To explain about databases, show the following video to the class: https://www.youtube.com/watch?v=Q2GMtIuaNzU. If needed, explain that specialists such as librarians cite and describe articles and other parts of a resource (such as a magazine or newspaper) as metadata and collect these metadata into databases. Database aggregators collect and index multiple databases to facilitate the retrieval of the metadata and often the information itself. Libraries subscribe to database aggregators because those products select age-appropriate materials and index them for easy retrieval.
3. To explain how to locate an article in an online database, show the following video to the class: https://www.youtube.com/watch?v= 6C3pOcbzUqQ. Also refer to http://libguides.mchenry.edu/ content.php?pid=528044&sid=4345522 as needed. Demonstrate a couple of sample searches from your library's database. If your school does not subscribe to any databases, contact the public library for access or use free databases, such as http://eric.ed.gov, or lists to them, such as http://csulb.libguides.com/freedatabases.
4. Ask students use a database in order to locate and cite two documents that help answer one of their research questions. Note that many databases now provide a standardized citation tool, which is usually accurate (students should review the citation because it is generated mechanically). Point out issues about citations as needed, using http://csulb.libguides.com/style. Then ask them to journal about their findings, comparing their results and processes used to locate, evaluate, and select.
5. If the class has access to several databases, discuss with them the process of choosing the most appropriate database by topic and the type of documents that the database indexes. Note that many databases provide information about their scope. Ask students to repeat the task with another database, if available and relevant. Then repeat the same tasks with the other research question.
6. Next, ask pairs to exchange their other research question with another pair, and repeat Step 5.
7. Debrief with the class about their experience in locating information: use of keywords, number of "hits," possible modifications of

searching, type of documents found, and the quality of the documents (e.g., currency, accuracy, reading level). "How does this experience inform your future online searching?"

Week 6: Researching the World Wide Web

1. Lead a class discussion about finding information on the Internet. Ask them how (e.g., using a search engine such as Google) and where (e.g., Wikipedia) they find information. Share the Power-Point http://www.schrockguide.net/uploads/3/9/2/2/392267/searching.pdf.
2. Ask students to search for their subject using two search engines and one search directory and compare the results (e.g., number of hits, order of results, types of resources).
3. Lead a class discussion about evaluating websites. Ask the class to list the criteria that they use to evaluate websites. Share the video https://www.commoncraft.com/video/website-evaluation.
4. Ask students in pairs to evaluate one of the websites listed on http://lib.nmsu.edu/instruction/evalexpl.html. Remind students to state the basis for their evaluation.
5. Ask students to locate and select two appropriate websites for their I-Search project. Ask them to cite and state the basis for their selection in their journal blog.

Week 7: Researching Encyclopedias and Dictionaries

1. General: State that this week marks the beginning of a section about reference "genres." For an overview, you can show the class this PowerPoint: http://www.cccc.edu/library/onlineresources/tutorials/files/PrintReference/files/PrintReference.ppt. Share this video about dictionaries, encyclopedias, and thesauri: https://www.youtube.com/watch?v=48IKfyP-Nug. (Note that it is for a younger audience but is still worthwhile, so view it ahead of time to see if your class will accept it.)
2. Provide the class with a variety of dictionaries, both print and digital. Ask students in pairs to examine a dictionary and list its general arrangement and entry-specific order (e.g., most common usage versus oldest usage first), its features (e.g., definition, pronunciation, usage, spellings, synonyms, origin/etymology, illustrations, appendixes such as rhymes), and its scope (e.g., abridged, unabridged, specific subject, visual, non-English, bilingual, gazetteer).

3. Ask students to give the class a 15-second "commercial" about their resource and its possible use (i.e., type of research question it could answer).
4. For the class, compare dictionaries and thesauri in terms of features and use for research. The latter helps generate additional keywords and can help in writing papers.
5. Ask students to search for their keywords or specialized topical terms in two dictionaries, and ask them to journal about their comparative findings.
6. Provide the class with a variety of encyclopedias, both print and digital. Ask students in pairs to examine an encyclopedia and list its general arrangement, article features (e.g., definition, history, illustrations, bibliography, length of article, cross-references), and its scope (e.g., general, specific subject).
7. Ask students to give the class a 15-second "commercial" about their resource and its possible use (i.e., type of research question it could answer).
8. Ask students to search for their keywords or specialized topical terms in two encyclopedias, and ask them to journal about their comparative findings.

Week 8: Time and Space Resources

1. Provide the class with an overview about the following reference types: "Time and space are important aspects of information. Statistics focuses on the numerical aspects of those factors. Statistical sources are largely found in almanacs, but there are many references that consist of numerical databases. Chronological reference gives info about historical and current dates. Atlases can encompass geography, politics, and history. There are also atlases of biomes and fantasy." Show this video on atlases and almanacs: https://www.youtube.com/watch?v=0AkhbhpdAKY. (Note that it is for a younger audience but is still worthwhile, so view it ahead of time to see if your class will accept it.)
2. Provide a variety of statistical, chronological, and atlas resources. Split the class in half, with one half critiquing statistical and chronological resources in pairs and the other half critiquing atlases. Alternatively, have the whole class in pairs critique each type, one after the other. Ask the pairs to list the general arrangement, article features, and scope.
3. Ask students to give the class a 15-second "commercial" about their resource and its possible use (i.e., type of research question it could answer).

4. Ask students to search for their keywords or specialized topical terms in two resources mentioned this week, and ask them to journal about their comparative findings.

Week 9: Resources About People

1. Provide the class with an overview about resources about people: "The first source of information is often another person. There are also many good references that give information about people: biographical, quotations (what they say), and directories (usually lists of groups)."
2. Provide a variety of resources about people. Ask the class in pairs to critique one resource, listing its general arrangement, article features, and scope.
3. Ask students to give the class a 15-second "commercial" about their resource and its possible use (i.e., type of research question it could answer).
4. Ask students to search for their keywords or specialized topical terms in one resource mentioned this week, and ask them to journal about their findings.

Week 10: Interviewing for Information

1. Lead a class discussion about interviewing: "When we have a question, we often ask someone for an answer. Learning how to interview someone—or a group of people—can be a good way to gain information. This skill is used by professionals and researchers too."
2. Ask students to interview someone about their research topic. If they don't know anyone, they can interview a librarian, who might have information or might be able to refer the student to an expert.
3. Lead a class discussion about this article: http://www.brighthubeducation.com/help-with-writing/97512-how-to-conduct-an-interview-for-a-paper/?cid=parsely_rec. Ask students how they might locate an expert. A good source is the librarian, who can probably locate good local informants.
4. Ask students to brainstorm a couple of experts, at least by title (e.g., professor, business person), for their research topic. Ask students to generate five to seven interview questions for those experts. Ask students to role play an informational research interview with a peer. Have pairs provide feedback about each other's expert and questions so that the originator can make improvements.

5. Ask students to locate and interview an expert, then journal their field notes and insights about their experience.

Week 11: Regrouping and Re-searching

1. Ask students to review their notes and journals in order to discern possible patterns, conflicting information, and gaps in information. Encourage them to organize their notes in some logical manner. Ask students what might be a logical way to organize their notes (e.g., time line, cause and effect, pro/con, thematic). Then ask them what kind of information matches each kind of organization.
2. Ask students to refer to the I-Search project rubric to guide their work. State: "When you start organizing and writing, information gaps and discrepancies may emerge. At that point, the citations come in handy because they help you retrieve resources and find more as needed. You also might need to alter the research questions in light of the information found." Also remind them to consult the bibliographies of resources already used. Encourage students to consult with a librarian to help them locate missing information. Remind students to consult their journal in terms of their experiences; good ideas might surface.

Week 12: Presenting Information

1. Lead a class discussion about presenting information. Students need to think about their content, the purpose of their presentation, their audience, and their time frame. In most cases, the purpose will be to inform and the audience will be the students' classmates.
2. Remind students that they need to write a report, which should include the information that they found, their interpretation of that information, and their conclusions, alongside their reflections on the process. Remind students that their report can include images and tables.

Week 13: Oral Presentation Tips

1. Students will also be asked to present their information orally in a 3-minute speech, explaining their process and their results.
2. Lead a class discussion about tips for doing oral presentations. Then share the following presentation tips: http://www. aresearchguide.com/3tips.html.
3. As a class, develop a checklist for oral presentations, or discuss an existing oral presentation checklist such as

Presenting:

- Good eye contact
- No *ums, like, you know*, "Am I making sense?"
- Appropriate speaking pace (a little slower than conversation)
- Speaking clearly, articulately, objectively, correctly
- Not reading strictly from notes
- Awareness of audience: align with venue's objective
- Responsive to audience verbally and using body language

Professionalism:

- Prepared
- Organized
- Appearance (attire, poise)
- Professional tone

Week 14: Project Presentation and Peer Review

1. Ask each student to orally present their I-Search project, and have two peers use the class oral presentation checklist to assess the presentation.
2. Ask students to journal about their experience presenting orally.

Week 15: Next Steps

1. Ask students to pair up and exchange their reports. Ask them to make comments using sticky notes.
2. Lead a class discussion about advice that they would give to the next class doing I-Search reports.
3. Ask students to review their journal blogs and write a final reflection about their experiences. What did they learn? What did they do well? What do they intend to improve?

CAPSTONE COURSE:
COMMUNITY-BASED ACTION RESEARCH PROJECT

The following community-based action research project course targets senior and advanced junior high schoolers and provides instruction in self-reflective research processes that involve a variety of information resources and tools. Educational technology is incorporated throughout the course in order for students to learn and apply the technology. It also enables students to conduct authentic action research that can improve their own environment. The course is designed as a full-semester offering, similar to a language arts course. If scaled down, it could be embedded into an existing course such as social studies. The librarian and classroom teacher can determine which content and activities are needed, depending on the student's prior knowledge and the context of the existing course.

Learning Objectives: Learners will

- assess themselves in terms of research processes
- develop an I-Search research project
- use a variety of research tools
- Communicate information effectively

Information Literacy Standards:

- Gain knowledge.
- Use and apply knowledge.
- Share knowledge.
- Pursue personal and esthetic growth.

Digital Literacy Standards:

- Use creative thinking and innovative technology.
- Use digital media and environments to communicate and collaborate.
- Apply digital tools fluently to plan, organize, and gather information in order to evaluate and analyze the information.
- Use critical thinking to research, manage projects, solve problems, and make informed decisions using technology.
- Practice digital citizenship.
- Use technology proficiently.

Common Core State Standards:

- Conduct research projects.
- Gather/assess information from multiple sources.
- Identify main ideas/themes and their development.
- Assess point of view and purpose in order to shape text content and style.
- Compare texts' content and approach.
- Read closely; cite evidence to support conclusions.
- Delineate/evaluate text arguments/claims and their reasoning.
- Evaluate/integrate content in different formats.
- Prepare/participate in range of conversations/collaborations.
- Draw evidence from texts to support analysis, reflection, and research.

- Use digital media/visual displays of data to express information/enhance understanding.
- Use technology to produce/publish writing and interact/collaborate.
- Write informative/explanatory texts.
- Write arguments in order to support claims.
- Produce clear, coherent writing.
- Use correct grammar and usage.
- Understand language functions in different contexts.
- Use correct spelling, punctuation, and capitalization.
- Use a range of academic and domain-specific words and phrases.
- Present information that listeners can follow.
- Adapt speech to various contexts and tasks.

Resources:

> Technology: Demo Internet-connected computer with data projector and screen; class set of Internet-connected computers, all of which should have the capability for online journaling/blogging.
>
> Handouts: Print out or otherwise make available handouts and other documents noted for each week (http://www.uk.sagepub.com/kumar4e/Kumar_Chapter_2.pdf).

Planning for Diverse Learners:

- Have students work in pairs (one typical and one with needs, such as language or physical limitations).
- Have students share equipment if there is limited access to it.
- Provide a choice of information sources.
- Provide more structure for the task or divide the steps into substeps.
- Topics may be sensitive for some students, so they should be able to choose their topics.

Assessments:

- Observe student participation and collaboration in terms of engagement, following directions, and communicating effectively.
- Assess students' decision-making processes and conclusions in terms of appropriateness and productivity.
- Critique student documentation in terms of following directions, the thoroughness and appropriateness of their notes and insights, and in terms of their writing skills.
- Observe students' technological competency in navigating the Internet, locating online resources, managing information, and using social media effectively and responsibly.

Instructional Strategies and Learning Activities:

Week 1: What Is Action Research?

1. Lead a class discussion about issues that students see in their school and community. Ask them what they can do about those issues.
2. Introduce the action research project: "The goal of the community-based action research project is to provide you with the opportunity to demonstrate your ability to critically examine selected issues in the community, review the relevant literature, gather data about the issue, develop a plan of action, and write an analysis based on your investigation. Ideally, the action research will lead to an actual intervention or project that is evaluated. You have the power to make a difference."
3. Walk through a sample action research project using the action research rubric below (table 8.3) (http://whatkidscando.org/specialcollections/student_research_action/index.html).
4. Ask students to analyze a sample action research project.

Week 2: What's a Good Research Question?

1. Ask students to identify two to three related issues to investigate. Ask them to create a concept map of the related issues, noting the problem, its impact and consequences, and possible reasons for the problem. Encourage them to jot down questions that might inform or contextualize the issue.
2. Lead a class discussion about asking research questions. Start with asking essential questions, a key problem to be solved that connects with the student. Lead the class in an exercise to determine the characteristics of an essential question: http://www.ascd.org/publications/books/109004/chapters/What-Makes-a-Question-Essential%A2.aspx.
3. Ask students to link their essential question to their concept map and generate some specific supporting questions to help flesh out their ideas and guide their work.
4. Ask students to generate some keywords for their essential and supporting questions.
5. Ask students to write a one-page essay on their action research issue, describing the problem and its context and explaining its significance.

Week 3: Looking for Insights

1. Lead a class discussion about looking for information about students' action research issue: "Where do you usually look for answers to problems you have?" (e.g., family, friends, experts, teachers, librarians, online, books, articles, media).

2. Explain that action research typically includes what other people have experienced, which might be recorded in print materials, online, and in the media. Researchers also gather data directly. "This week you will be reviewing the efforts and research that other people have done about your issue—a literature review. Note that you might need to locate information that is more general. For instance, if you're concerned about school bathrooms, you might need to look at bathroom conditions in public buildings."

3. Encourage students to search in a variety of documentation and to focus on articles from reputable journals found in subscription database aggregators (http://www.youtube.com/watch?v= KKIbnNLCh8g). Review how to find articles (http://libguides. mchenry.edu/content.php?pid=528044&sid=4345522), cite sources (http://csulb.libguides.com/style), and take notes (http:// library.sasaustin.org/noteTaking.php).

4. With the class, review how to evaluate websites (https://www. commoncraft.com/video/website-evaluation).

Week 4: Synthesizing the Literature Review

1. Ask students to review their notes in order to discern possible patterns, conflicting information, and gaps in information. Encourage them to organize their notes in some logical manner. Explain that most literature reviews organize information thematically.

2. Ask students to refer to the action research project rubric to guide their work. State: "When you start organizing and writing, information gaps and discrepancies may emerge. At that point, the citations come in handy because it helps you retrieve resources and find more as needed. You also might need to alter the research questions in light of the information found." Also remind them to consult bibliographies of resources already used. Encourage students to consult with a librarian to help them locate missing information.

Week 5: Gathering Data With Instruments

1. Lead a class discussion about gathering data for students' action research. Explain that data are needed to describe the current situation: people, behaviors, attitudes, settings, resources, time frame.

2. Ask students to review their questions and identify the information that they want. Ask students to translate the information into data (and data points).

3. Lead a class discussion about data collection instruments, using http://betterevaluation.org/plan/describe/collect_retrieve_data. For each collection method, ask students to suggest an example that they might use for their action research project.

4. Ask students to choose two to three data collection instruments and list the data that they want to collect.

Week 6: Observation and Content Analysis

1. Lead a class discussion about observing people, places, and processes, trying not to interfere with the setting. Explain that technology can help capture details: cameras for still images and camcorders for continuous action. Explain that observation involves making field notes about what students see and experience.

2. Ask students to observe their class for 5 minutes. Ask students to pair-share their field notes.

3. Debrief with the class about what was observed, what data they collected, and how they kept notes.

4. Ask students to analyze their field notes and make inferences about their observations. "What patterns, trends, and distinguishing factors did you observe? What data supports your interpretation?"

5. Explain that content analysis resembles observation in that patterns, trends, and distinguishing factors are identified when reviewing existing documents.

6. Ask students to analyze their school yearbook for 5 minutes. Ask students to pair-share their notes and interpretations.

7. Debrief with the class about what was observed, what data they collected, how they kept notes, and their interpretations.

8. Ask students to choose at least one situation to observe and one to two documents to analyze and list the data that they want to collect.

Week 7: Focus Groups

1. Explain about focus groups: asking a group of people about their perspectives in terms of thoughts, actions, and attitudes. "Focus groups are a good way to see what issues emerge."

2. With the class, walk through one of these guides to focus groups: http://www.webcredible.com/blog-reports/web-usability/focus-

groups.shtml or https://www.nationalgangcenter.gov/Content/ Documents/Assessment-Guide/Assessment-Guide-Chapter-9.pdf.

3. Ask the class to role play a focus group session and debrief their experience.

4. Ask students to identify a list of appropriate focus group participants for their action research project and generate a set of questions. Ask students to pair off and evaluate each other's lists.

5. Ask students to plan and implement a focus group related to their research topic.

Week 8: Surveys

1. Surveys gather data about people. Questionnaires are sets of questions.

2. Walk through http://www.socialresearchmethods.net/kb/survey. htm.

3. Ask students to locate and take a survey, ideally related to their action research topic, and critique it.

4. Ask students to identify a list of appropriate focus group participants for their action research project and generate a set of questions. Ask students to pair off and evaluate each other's surveys.

5. Encourage students to locate applicable surveys (usually found in research articles) and adapt them rather than creating their own from scratch. Published surveys are usually validated so that the data collected relates to the issue being investigated.

Week 9: Interviews

1. Lead a class discussion about interviewing: "When we have a question, we often ask someone for an answer. Learning how to interview someone—or a group of people—can be a good way to gain information. This skill is often used by professionals and researchers. Individual interviews are useful for discovering the reason for survey findings."

2. Ask students to interview someone about their research topic. If they don't know anyone, they can interview a librarian, who might have information or might be able to refer the student to an expert.

3. Lead a class discussion about this article: http://www. brighthubeducation.com/help-with-writing/97512-how-to-conduct-an-interview-for-a-paper/?cid=parsely_rec. Ask students how they might locate an expert; a good source is the librarian, who can probably locate local good informants.

4. Ask students to brainstorm a couple of experts, at least by title (e.g., professor, business person), for their action research topic. Ask students to generate five to seven interview questions for those experts. Ask students to role play an informational research interview with a peer. Have the pairs provide feedback about each other's expert and questions so that the originator can make improvements.
5. Ask students to locate and interview an expert, then take field notes and draw insights about their experience.

Week 10: Analyzing Data

1. Lead a class discussion about analyzing data: "Analysis identifies the trends and discrepancies and seeks reasons for the findings." With the class, walk through the points at http://betterevaluation. org/plan/describe/look_for_patterns. State: "By now you have collected data and done some analysis of the findings. Use some of the techniques mentioned in the website to analyze your data systematically."
2. Ask students to compare their data from different sources and figure out how to resolve discrepancies. Remind them to draw on their literature review in order to help them analyze their data.
3. Encourage students to visualize their findings. With the class walk through http://betterevaluation.org/plan/describe/visualise_data.

Week 11: Drawing Conclusions

1. Ask students to align their research questions, their literature review, their data, and their analysis. Ask, "What is the story that emerges?"
2. Ask students to write their conclusions in essay form, backing up their stance with their literature review and data.

Week 12: Making Recommendations

1. Explain that the main goal of action research is improvement: "At this point, you have described the issue and figured out the reasons for the problem and ways to solve it. Now is the time to take your conclusions and transform them into actions."
2. With the class, walk through http://www.researchtoaction.org/ 2013/07/how-to-write-actionable-policy-recommendations/.
3. Ask students to write up their recommendations and have a peer critique them.

Week 13: Making an Action Plan

1. Lead a class discussion about making an action plan by turning their recommendations into action.
2. With the class, walk through http://ctb.ku.edu/en/table-of-contents/ structure/strategic-planning/develop-action-plans/main.
3. Ask students to write up their action plan and have a peer critique it.

Week 14: Communicating Your Ideas

1. Lead a class discussion about tips for doing oral presentations. Share the following presentation tips: http://www.aresearchguide. com/3tips.html.
2. As a class, develop a checklist for oral presentations or discuss an existing oral presentation checklists such as:

   Presenting:

   - Good eye contact
   - No *ums, like, you know,* "Am I making sense?"
   - Appropriate speaking pace (a little slower than conversation)
   - Speaking clearly, articulately, objectively, and correctly
   - Not reading strictly from notes
   - Awareness of the audience: align with the venue's objective
   - Responsive to audience verbally and through body language

   Professionalism:

   - Prepared
   - Organized
   - Appearance (attire, poise)
   - Professional tone

3. Ask students to present their action research orally in a 3-minute speech, explaining their process and their results. Encourage them to use visualizations.

Week 15: Final Report: Format Guidelines

All pages must be typed, double-spaced, consecutively numbered, and printed on only one side of the page. Use 1-inch margins, and 12-point font (Times Roman, Arial, or Calibri). A maximum length of 25 pages of text (excluding references and attachments) is expected.

Introduction of the action research problem: include description, context, and need.

Elements:

- Literature review that shows how the problem has been researched and addressed
- Pose the research questions
- Methodology that describes what data the student collected and how he or she collected it (have at least two tools) as he or she investigated the problem/issue
- Findings of data collected
- Discussion of the findings (analyze the data and what it means)
- Recommendations for addressing the problem
- Action plan: The student should describe what action he or she would take, how he or she would measure its impact, and its potential contributions to professional practice. This section may also include a time line, budget, a statement of deliverables, and what the final work product will be if a project is being proposed.

Student assessments appear in table 8.3.

Table 8.3. Action Research Rubric

	4	3	2	1
Topic	Action research topic and problem are very clearly defined.	Action research topic is adequately defined.	Action research topic is vague and poorly defined.	Action research topic is not defined.
Problem	Thorough identification of factors and a clear determination of relative influence of each variable are given.	Factors and influence of each variable are identified.	Some obvious factors are missing and no relative influences are identified.	Little identification of factors is apparent.
Literature Review	Literature review analyzes, prioritizes, and synthesizes	Literature review analyzes and synthesizes main factors	Literature review addresses main factors, though not in	Literature review is superficial or off-target.

	4	3	2	1
	factors clearly and insightfully.	clearly.	depth.	
Methodology	Thorough description of plan of action/ methodology based on prior research and problem analysis.	Plan of action/ methodology described and justified.	Plan of action/ methodology described.	Poor methodology.
Data Collection	Used two valid, reliable data-collection strategies; data clearly compared with literature review.	Used a valid, reliable data-collection strategy; data compared with literature review.	Used a valid, reliable data-collection strategy.	No valid, reliable data collected.
Data Analysis	Data are described and analyzed clearly and accurately; conflicting findings are resolved.	Data are described and analyzed at a basic level.	Data are described.	Little data are provided.
Action Plan	Action plans are clearly explained based on collected data and literature review.	Action plans are somewhat explained and based on collected data and literature review.	Action plan is based on "best guess" as it related somewhat to collected data.	Action plan makes little sense; no data connected.
Writing	College-level work: clear organization, well written, few/no mechanical errors.	Senior-level work: generally well written, satisfactory organization.	Junior-level work: adequate writing but unclear, some mechanical errors.	Sophomore-level work: unclear, unorganized writing; many mechanical errors.
Total Points				

IMPLICATIONS FOR SCHOOL LIBRARIANS

School librarians have a special responsibility to make sure that all students gain information and digital competence by the time they graduate. For some students, high school may be the last time that they have formal education experiences. High school graduates (and those who do not graduate) need these skills in order to continue their learning independently and through informal education, regardless of their work and personal settings. School librarians can have valuable discussions with seniors and graduates one year out in order to determine what curriculum helped them and what changes should be made in order to optimize learning and application of information and digital literacies.

Bibliography

Agosto, D. (2011). Young adults' information behavior: What we know so far and where we need to go from here. *Journal of Research on Libraries and Young Adults, 2*(1). Retrieved from http://www.yalsa.ala.org/jrlya/2011/11/young-adults%E2%80%99-information-behavior-what-we-know-so-far-and-where-we-need-to-go-from-here/

American Association of School Librarians. (2009). *Standards for the 21st century learner in action.* Chicago, IL: American Library Association.

American Association of School Librarians. (2007). *Standards for the 21st century learner.* Chicago, IL: American Library Association.

American Association of School Librarians and Achieve. (2013). *Implementing the Common Core State Standards: The role of the school librarian.* Chicago, IL: American Library Association.

American Library Association Presidential Committee on Information Literacy. (1989). *Final report.* Chicago, IL: American Library Association.

Association for Childhood Education International. (2007). *Elementary education standards and supporting explanation.* Washington, DC: Association for Childhood Education International.

Association of College and Research Libraries. (2015). *Framework for Information literacy for higher education.* Chicago, IL: American Library Association.

Association of College and Research Libraries. (2012). *Characteristics of programs of information literacy that illustrate best practices.* Chicago, IL: American Library Association.

Association of College and Research Libraries. (2000). *Information literacy competency standards for higher education.* Chicago, IL: American Library Association.

Belshaw, D. (2011). *What is digital literacy? A pragmatic investigation* (Doctoral dissertation). Durham University, Durham, UK.

Board on Science Education. Division of Behavioral and Social Sciences and Education. National Research Council of the National Academies. (2012). *A framework for K–12 science education.* Washington, DC: National Academies Press.

Branch, J. (2001). Information-seeking processes of junior high school students. *School Libraries Worldwide, 7*(1), 11–27.

Branson, R., & Rayner, G. (1975). *Interservice procedures for instructional systems development.* Tallahassee: Center for Educational Technology, Florida State University.

California State Department of Education. (2011). *Model school library standards for California public schools: Kindergarten through grade twelve.* Sacramento, CA: California State Department of Education.

Chen, S., & Fu, Y. (2009). Internet use and academic achievement: Gender differences in early adolescence. *Adolescence, 44*(176), 797–812.

Common Sense Media. (2013). *Zero to eight: Children's media use in America 2013*. San Francisco, CA: Common Sense Media.

Council of Chief State School Officers and the National Governors Association. (2010). *The Common Core State Standards for English language arts & literacy in history/social studies, science, and technical subjects*. Washington, DC: Common Core State Standards Initiative.

Dobbs, D. (2011). Beautiful brains. *National Geographic, 220*(4), 37–59.

Domer, D., & Gorman, G. (2006). Information literacy education in Asian developing countries: Cultural factors affecting curriculum development and programme delivery. *IFLA Journal, 32*(4), 281–293.

Feierabend, S., & Rathgeb, T. (2012). Media usage behaviour of adolescents in Germany. *Media Perspektiven, 43*(6), 339–352.

File, T., & Ryan, C. (2014). *Computer and Internet use in the United States: 2013*. Washington, DC: U.S. Census Bureau.

Flanagan, A., & Metzger, M. (2010). *Kids and credibility: An empirical examination of youth, digital media use, and information credibility*. Cambridge, MA: MIT Press.

Foss, E. (2014). *Internet searching in children and adolescents: A longitudinal framework of youth search roles* (Doctoral dissertation). University of Maryland, College Park, MD.

Fresno County Office of Education. (n.d.). *Technology standards*. Fresno, CA: Fresno County Office of Education.

Friedman, T. (2005). *The world is flat*. New York: Farrar, Straus and Giroux.

Gardner, H. (1983). *Frames of mind: The theory of multiple intelligences*. New York: Basic Books.

Gasser, U., Cortesi, S., Malik, M., & Lee, A. (2012). *Youth and digital media: From credibility to information quality*. Cambridge, MA: Berkman Center for Internet & Society.

Gilster, P. (1997). *Digital literacy*. New York: Wiley.

Hubbell, E. (2010). Using McREL's knowledge taxonomy for ed tech professional development. *Learning & Leading with Technology, 37*(8), 20–23.

ICT Literacy Panel. (2002). *Digital transformation: A framework for ICT literacy*. Princeton, NJ: Educational Testing Service.

International Society for Technology in Education. (2007a). *International educational technology standards for students*. Eugene, OR: International Society for Technology in Education.

International Society for Technology in Education. (2007b). *Profiles for technology (ICT) literate students*. Eugene, OR: International Society for Technology in Education.

International Technology Education Association. (2007). *Standards for technological literacy: Content for the study of technology* (3rd ed.). Reston, VA: International Technology Education Association.

Keeble, L., & Loader, B. (2001). *Social capital and cyberpower*. London: Routledge.

Kolb, D. (1984). *Experiential learning: Experiences as the source of learning and development*. Englewood Cliffs, NJ: Prentice-Hall.

Lien, C. (2000). Approaches to Internet searching: An analysis of student in grades 2 to 12. *Journal of Instruction Delivery Systems, 14*(3), 6–13.

Lu, Y. (2010). Children's information seeking in coping with daily-life problems: An investigation of fifth- and sixth-grade students. *Library & Information Science Research, 32*, 77–88.

Lubans, J. (1999). When students hit the surf: What kids really do on the Internet. And what they want from librarians. *School Library Journal, 45*(9), 144–147.

Madden, M., Lenhart, A., Duggan, M., Cortesi, K., & Gasser, U. (2013). *Teens and technology 2013*. Washington, DC: Pew Research Center.

Marzano, R., Marzano, J., & Pickering, D. (2003). *Classroom management that works*. Alexandria, VA: Association of Supervision and Curriculum Development.

Mishra, P., & Koehler, M. (2006). Technological pedagogical content knowledge: A framework for teacher knowledge. *Teachers College Record, 108*(6), 1017–1054.

Montiel-Overall, P. (2005). A theoretical understanding of TLC. *School Libraries Worldwide, 11*(2), 24–48.

National Council for Accreditation of Teacher Education. (2008). *Unit standards in effect*. Washington, DC: National Council for Accreditation of Teacher Education.

Nevison, J. (1976, October 22). Computing in the liberal arts college. *Science*, 396–402.

Oakleaf, M., & Owen, P. (2010). Closing the 12–13 gap together: School and college librarians supporting 21st century learners. *Teacher Librarian, 37*(4), 52–58.

Office for Information Technology Policy. (2013). *Digital literacy, libraries, and public policy*. Chicago, IL: American Library Association.

Partnership for 21st Century Skills. (2013). *Reimagining citizenship for the 21st century*. Washington, DC: Partnership for 21st Century Skills.

Perry, W. (1999). *Forms of intellectual and ethical development in the college years*. San Francisco, CA: Jossey-Bass.

Purcell, K., Rainie, L., Heaps A., Buchanan, J., Friedrich, L., Jacklin, A., Chen, C., Zickuhr, K. (2012). *How teens do research in the digital world*. Washington, DC: Pew Internet & American Life Project. Retrieved from http://pewinternet.org/~/media//Files/Reports/2012PIP_TeacherSurveyReportWithMethodology110112.pdf

Ribble, M. (2011). *Digital citizenship in schools* (2nd ed.). Eugene, OR: International Society for Technology in Education.

Rideout, V., Foehr, U., & Roberts, D. (2010). *Generation M2: Media in the lives of 8- to 18-year-olds*. Menlo Park, CA: Kaiser Family Foundation.

Savolainen, Reijo, & Kari, Jarkko. (2004). Placing the Internet in information source horizons. *Library and Information Science Research, 26*, 415–433.

Search Institute. (2007). *40 developmental assets for adolescents*. Minneapolis, MN: Search Institute. Retrieved from http://www.search-institute.org/content/40-developmental-assets-adolescents-ages-12-18

Smaldino, S., & Lowther, D. (2011). *Instructional technology and media for learning* (10th ed.). Upper Saddle River, NJ: Pearson.

Sternberg, R. (1985). *Beyond IQ: A triarchic theory of human intelligence*. Cambridge, MA: Harvard University Press.

UNESCO. (2014). *Global media and information assessment framework: Country readiness and competencies*. The Hague, Netherlands: UNESCO.

United Nations. (2003). *Declaration of principles. Building the information society: A global challenge in the new millennium*. Paris, France: United Nations.

United Nations. (1948). *Universal declaration of human rights*. Paris, France: United Nations.

United States Department of Education. (1983). *A nation at risk*. Washington, DC: Government Printing Office.

Vansickle, S. (2002). Tenth graders' search knowledge and use of the web. *Knowledge Quest, 30*(4), 33–37.

Wang, L., Luo, J., Gao, W., & Kong, J. (2012). The effect of Internet use on adolescents' lifestyles. *Computers in Human Behavior, 28*(6), 2007–2013.

Wartberg, L., Kammerl, R., Sonja Bröning, S., Hauenschild, M., Petersen, K., & Thomasius, R. (2014). Gender-related consequences of Internet use perceived by parents in a representative quota sample of adolescents. *Behaviour & Information Technology*. doi: 10.1080/0144929X.2014.928746

Zickuhr, K., Rainie, L., & Purcell, K. (2013). *Library services in the digital age*. Washington, DC: Pew Research Center.

Zurkowski, P. (1974). *The information service environment—Relationships and priorities*. Washington, DC: U.S. Commission on Libraries and Information Science.

Index

About the Author

Lesley S. J. Farmer, professor at California State University, Long Beach, coordinates the librarianship program. She earned her MS in library science at the University of North Carolina, Chapel Hill, and received her doctorate in adult education from Temple University. Farmer has worked as a teacher librarian in K–12 school settings, as well as in public, special, and academic libraries. She is past chair of the education section of the Special Libraries Association, edits two International Federation of Library Associations and Institutions (IFLA) section blogs, and is a Fulbright scholar. In 2011, she was selected for the American Library Association (ALA) Beta Phi Mu Award for contributions to library education and was recently awarded the Library Instruction Round Table (LIRT) Librarian Recognition Award. She is a frequent presenter and writer for the profession, and her research interests include information literacy, collaboration, assessment, and educational technology.